Books by Amanda Bennett

AUTHOR

The Death of the Organization Man

COAUTHOR

The Man Who Stayed Behind

The Quiet Room

IN MEMORIAM

A PRACTICAL GUIDE
TO PLANNING
A MEMORIAL SERVICE

AMANDA BENNETT
& TERENCE B. FOLEY

A FIRESIDE BOOK
PUBLISHED BY SIMON & SCHUSTER

FIRESIDE
Rockefeller Center
1230 Avenue of the Americas
New York, NY 10020

Copyright © 1997 by Amanda Bennett and Terence B. Foley

Designed by Jenny Dossin

Manufactured in the United States of America

1 3 5 7 9 10 8 6 4 2

Library of Congress Cataloging-in-Publication Data

Bennett, Amanda.
In memoriam : a practical guide to planning a memorial service /
Amanda Bennett & Terence Foley
p.   cm.
"A Fireside book."
Includes bibliographical references and index.
1. Memorial service.   I. Foley, Terence B.   II. Title.
BV199.M4B38   1997
393'.9—dc21   97-8972
CIP
ISBN 0-684-81902-3

FOR N.M.W. AND R.F.R.

CONTENTS

INTRODUCTION

There are few events in life we face with more apprehension than the funeral of someone we love. At the same time, there are few urges more profound than the need to commemorate our loved ones, to celebrate their lives, and to mourn their passing.

Every culture has its rituals marking the passage from life; nearly every religion has its rite honoring the dead. Some of the world's most moving poems have been funeral elegies, some of the world's most beautiful music has been written for requiem services, and some of history's most stirring speeches have been funeral orations. The poems and music lament the sting of death and sing of the joy of life. The religious rites ease the passage of the spirit to the next world.

But despite our desire to commemorate, we often face the task of planning funerals and memorial services with dread. That is understandable. The ceremonies that mark life's other major passages—such as weddings and christenings—are filled with joy and hope. Funerals and memorial services, by contrast, are almost inevitably tinged with grief, even for the most devout believer in another, better world to come.

Moreover, weddings and christenings, birthdays, anniversaries, bar and bas mitzvahs can all be planned at leisure over a long period of time. But while some people plan their memorial services ahead of time, the majority do not, so others must do it for them. Thus, most funerals and memorial services are conceived and executed at moments of great stress and under extreme time pressures.

Even so, the scores of people we interviewed in the preparation of this book recalled with thankfulness the services they helped plan for their spouses, parents, siblings, and friends. Many were surprised to discover just how much satisfaction they found in these rites. In the months and years following, they frequently returned with pleasure to the memories of these services. Among those whose memories were less pleasant, however, the reason was never that they found the occasion too mournful. Rather, they regretted that the press of time, their own bereavement, or simply lack of imagination or resources had kept them from creating a suitable service.

What made the difference?

Those who were satisfied felt that the service they had created was appropriate to the person who died. That it was beautiful. That it expressed to the family and to the community who the person was, why his life was important, and how much he would be missed.

For some people, that meant taking refuge in tradition. For them, the comforting cadences of centuries-old religious rites plus the familiarity of old hymns and of a priest preaching the promise of resurrection were consoling. But many other people found the most satisfaction in personalizing a service, in making a service that memorialized this person and no other. They shared stories of the person's life, praised his accomplishments, explained his aspirations. They played his music and told his jokes. In either case, the services that were the most uplifting were the ones that were planned with much thought and care.

What is the purpose of a funeral or memorial service? Why this need to hold a formal service of commemoration? What does this public rite accomplish that private grieving can't? What end do funerals and memorial services serve?

Because the funeral marks the end of the life of the body, historically one function has been a sacramental one. In many religions, at least one major function of the funeral is to ease the passage of the dead to the next world. Thus, the living gather to offer their prayers of assistance. Buddhists chant sutras to help direct the spirit; Catholics pray souls out of Purgatory.

But even nonreligious funerals have at their very base a profound feeling of social and moral obligation to the dead. In Sophocles' play, Antigone goes to her own death for disobeying her uncle's orders and refusing to let her brother lie unburied. It is that deep sense that no one should leave the earth unmemorialized that led one priest we interviewed to conduct a memorial service alone in an empty chapel for an elderly man who had outlived everyone else who might have remembered and mourned his passing. It is that same sense of obligation to the dead that leads us to come from great distances to attend the funeral of someone we loved or admired.

A memorial service—in contrast to a funeral—accomplishes that aim not by focusing on the passage of the person who died to the next world but by centering on a remembrance of his life. A memorial service is seen not as a dirge for a life that has passed but as a commemoration of a life well lived.

As we will see in later chapters, both funerals and memorial services are becoming increasingly less mournful. More and more people are choosing cheerful, upbeat music and poems of inspiration rather than of mourning. The eulogies may be filled with humor, and a ceremony may stress hope and the continuation of life in the aftermath of death.

Indeed, both funerals and memorial services are now often spoken of as "celebrations." Moreover, there is an increasing recognition that services for the dead are actually services for the living. Even when they are focused on the person who has died, their purpose is to help those left behind come to terms with death and go on with life.

How do they do that? For one thing, funerals and memorial services serve to gather a community around the grieving family and friends. There is nothing more consoling to those nearest to the person who has died than to realize how much their loved one was loved by others. Often it even comes as a surprise to the family to discover just how far afield the person's influence had spread. When old teachers, former students, bosses, colleagues, shopkeepers, college classmates, and sports teammates share in a funeral or memorial service, they provide a reassuring presence for those closest to him.

For those in that extended community, too, a well-planned memorial service provides a fuller picture of a person's entire life. We may have known our friend professionally but never knew that he had once been a fighter pilot. We may have played ball alongside him for years without realizing that he had a master's degree in French literature. We may not have known that our college classmate had worked regularly in a homeless shelter. Or that the person we thought of as our little cousin had gone on to achieve such professional acclaim. We often live geographically, professionally, and socially fragmented lives; in the stories told by others, we can assemble those fragments into a picture of a whole life and a whole person.

Nonetheless, no one should overlook the age-old, traditional role of the funeral, which is to provide an occasion for the bereaved to mourn and to be comforted. In most memorial services, people shy away from talk of death, dying, grief, and mourning, but they should not, in their focus on life, overlook the weight of grief that loved ones are bearing.

The best of all services make it possible for people both to express their love and pride in the life of the deceased and to talk about their deep feelings of loss. "I believe a memorial service makes it easier to bear the grief of a loved one's passing," said one Atlanta woman whose husband died of AIDS. While the focus of her husband's service, she said, was "remember the good times," she and her family were also able to talk freely about their loss. "My little girl was able to express what she and her daddy were like together and what she felt about that."

Finally, a memorial service can provide an example to everyone who attends. We can leave a profoundly moving service thinking about what is worthwhile in our own lives: What is important? What is unimportant? What would people say about our lives? What would we want them to say?

By necessity, when a death occurs, your first thoughts must be about the disposition of the body and its eventual resting place. For that reason, we have described the choices available to you in the Appendix, "Basic Funeral Planning." Once these decisions have been made, however, you can turn your thoughts to how you wish to memorialize the deceased. The purpose of this book is to lay out in a simple, matter-of-fact way everything you need to know to create the best memorial service possible for your loved one or to guide you in leaving instructions for your own. We have tried to provide a wide range of examples, culled from the experiences of people all over the country and drawn from memorial services for people who lived to a full old age as well as from those for people who—as a result of illness or accident—were forced to leave their lives far too soon.

Some of the services were held for famous and much-lauded people, attended by celebrities and written about by the press. Others were services for people the world would consider unimportant—accountants and bankers, lawyers and construction workers. They were Masons, Catholics, Baptists, and atheists. The services were held in cathedrals and chapels, in funeral homes and art museums. They took place on golf courses, in bowling alleys, and thousands of feet in the air.

Some of the memorial services we describe had few attendees. Others were attended by thousands of mourners. The service for one ninety-seven-year-old rural man was attended by 650 people, showing the surprising reach of ordinary lives—the church from which he was buried had 100 members, and the man was related to all of them.

Some of the services were for people who were clearly well loved and provided opportunities for those who attended to express their love. Others, for people who all their lives had caused pain to those around them, were aimed at healing. The much-publicized memorial service for film director Louis Malle showed how even the families of the famous must deal with the pain both of their loved ones' deaths and of their own lives.

The service we attended for one woman who had passed her life as a barkeeper unexpectedly offered moving lessons in the light that radiates from seemingly obscure lives. At this woman's service, person after person stood to speak of their childhoods spent in her home. They told of how she had rescued them from the streets, taken them in, fed them, clothed them, and sent them to church. They all wondered what would have become of them had it not been for her love and care.

All the services we have written about had something special about them. Each one expressed the personality of an individual and the importance of his or her life to others. We believe that everyone's life has this unique beauty, and we have written this guide to help you find it, present it to others, and take comfort from it yourself.

IN
MEMORIAM

CHAPTER ONE

THE FIRST STEPS
IN PLANNING A SERVICE

A memorial service for someone we love begins not with the service itself but with the planning for it. Indeed, one of the gifts of a funeral or memorial service is that in those crucial first days after the death of a loved one, it forces people to focus their thoughts and emotions on planning something positive. Memorializing a person—even a person who was very near and dear—means having to think hard about that person and to examine the meaning of her life and the role she played in others' lives. It means coming face-to-face with her values—and our own.

The reminiscing, evaluating, and weighing that take place in the planning of the service can be important in itself as part of the process of grieving and healing. Moreover, it is from the things that are discovered in the process that a memorable and moving service grows.

For most people, this process begins within the first day or so after the death. As you think through the life of the person you are going to memorialize, you will find that the outlines of a potential service will quickly emerge. Some aspects will be determined by the depth of her religious faith, for example, or of her love of a certain kind of music or flowers or poetry. Other aspects will be determined by your family, your community, your geographic location, and your own creative and artistic skills.

The first thing to do, then, is to sit down, pencil and paper in hand, and begin to plan. If you find that doing this job alone is an impossible task, ask someone to help you. Close relatives, of course, will have suggestions and thoughts. Many people consult their pastor, priest, or rabbi or a funeral home director for specific assistance. Such people can help with the planning and also provide spiritual and emotional solace. A funeral director is well prepared to provide advice of a more practical nature.

But it is friends, family, and associates who will actually be the most help in preparing the service. You might simply turn to a friend of the family who, while close, is less emotionally devastated. In most cases, one person—a spouse, a close friend, a son or daughter, brother or sister—will become the main focus of all the planning efforts.

In some cases, you may have to limit the number of people who want to participate. "If there are too many people involved in the planning, it becomes a problem. It leads to competition among people to manage the service," said the Reverend Thomas Pellaton, a priest at Saint Michael's Episcopal Church in New York. There will, of course, be many different tastes to accommodate and the feelings of many different people to consider. But planning the memorial service shouldn't turn into a battle among competing groups.

Still, don't overlook the fact that help may come from unexpected places. As word of the death spreads, people will emerge who may be quite unknown to you but who played key roles in your loved one's life. This will be especially true if the person you are memorializing lived in a different part of the country. For example, when Deborah Lewine flew from New York to California to help plan her brother Jeff's service, she got a great deal of help from the captain of his softball team, who knew her brother and his friends well.

You may be reluctant to ask someone for such help. You may feel that it is a tremendous burden and an imposition. Ask anyway. Planning a memorial service is an intimate and personal job, and people you ask to help may be honored because, at such a time, they want to feel close and needed.

Your decision about the kind of service you choose to create will rest in part on your own needs and preferences and in part on the needs and preferences of others who will participate. But all planning should begin with thoughtful consideration of the person to be memorialized.

WHO WAS THE PERSON WHO DIED?

You may think you knew the person well—especially if he or she was a person very dear to you—but the answer to this question may not be as easy as it first appears. In fact, the closer you were to the person, the more difficult it may be to answer. If your understanding of a person is based on familiarity and habit, it may take some thought to single out those characteristics that will have the most meaning to others.

You and the people who are helping you should first think about what kind of a person your loved one was: Was she socially active, or were friends and family her chief interest? How would other people have described her? When preparing a memorial service, think about what kind of a service would best fit her personality. Was she a casual, informal person, the kind you could drop in on for an impromptu chat? Or was she a formal, dignified person who put great stock in appearances and proprieties? Whatever the answer, the service should be planned to reflect not just the realities of the person's life but the tone of that life as well. We discovered moving, beautiful services of great majesty and dignity; we also found rollicking services full of merriment and joking. In both cases, they reflected the personality of the people who had died and of their position in the community. Perhaps the person lived her life to shock and confound those around her; if so, an offbeat service filled with iconoclastic readings and lively music might be just the thing. But if she lived within the mores of her own community, you should take those standards into consideration.

Who were her close friends? Her acquaintances? Her business associates? Will you be planning a service for a large group of people drawn from many different, unrelated groups? Or did she live her life largely within her own community? The tone of the service will be determined, in part, by whether you are sharing the details of a life with a small group of close friends or tying together the details of a life lived among many different kinds of people. If your service is to include eulogies, you will also want to consider who among her friends you will want to speak. (Chapter 8, "The Eulogy," gives specific suggestions on choosing who will speak and on helping them decide what to say.)

What kinds of books and periodicals did she read? A service for someone who regularly read *Rolling Stone* should be different from a service for someone who steeped herself in Blake. Many religions restrict the breadth of readings allowed. But in a secular service, your choice is unlimited (Chapters 2, 11, and 12 discuss readings for memorial services.)

What kind of music did she listen to or perform? The music played at a service can be very evocative, particularly if it is strongly associated with the person who has died. Is there a song she used to sing? Some music that everyone in her group will find familiar? Again, the choices may be limited in religious services but can be unlimited in secular services. (Chapter 13, "Music for the Service," offers suggestions for how to choose appropriate music as well as selections from a wide variety of musical traditions.)

Did the person have any special hobbies or skills? Consider assembling a collage or a "memory table" to honor those abilities. (See Chapter 6, "Planning an Informal, Creative service," for possibilities.) One person who recently planned a memorial service for a relative went through his personal files and found a résumé which proved very helpful. Such a résumé would, at a glance, remind you of all the different places in which that person had lived and worked. It would also be invaluable in writing an obituary and sending it to papers in the different communities where he had lived and for notifying employers and former employers.

While some of your insights, thoughts, and remembrances of the person who has died will immediately seem important, don't overlook things that at first blush seem trivial.

Take, for example, the memorial service for Nina Weisse of Framingham, Massachusetts. It was a rather conventional Catholic service, except for one special aspect that stemmed from her relatives' recollections of her. All her life, Nina had surrounded herself with soft colors. Nearly all of her friends associated her—petite and pretty even at eighty-three—with pastels. So relatives banned all black and instead planned everything in shades of pink, yellow, and light green. No one today remembers much about the service itself. But when they remember seeing the lavender hearse, hired especially for the occasion, those who loved her smile and say, "That was Nina!"

DID HE LEAVE INSTRUCTIONS?

Many people leave at least sketchy indications of their preferences for funerals or memorial services tucked in with their wills or other important papers. They can be as simple as a note about favorite music or flowers, or they can be quite elaborate plans. Some people pick the location for the service, choose the minister or other celebrant, select the music and readings, and even designate which of their friends will play which role. Because of the long time they often have in anticipation of death, those stricken with AIDS, in particular, sometimes plan quite thoroughly for their own services. Many have said that it helped them focus on their own lives, what they had accomplished and what they had left undone. Many of their plans are for exuberant celebrations filled with music and readings and provide specific roles for the friends who shared their lives.

But even older people whose services are steeped in tradition take satisfaction from thorough planning. When she died at age ninety-three, Mrs. Charles H. Battle of Atlanta left behind elaborate instructions. "She planned everything," Lola Battle, her daughter-in-law, recalled. "She specified the memorial service, the coffin, the funeral home—she enjoyed planning all that. She was a great one for planning and directing. She was the family matriarch and normally had planned everything." The result was a sweet but simple Baptist service. "Probably her only regret," Lola Battle said, "was that she couldn't be present to make sure the memorial service went all right."

It's important to look for any instructions the deceased may have left. It would be a shame to stumble across them weeks later and to feel that, even accidentally, the deceased's wishes had not been carried out. Most people find it emotionally satisfying to follow such instructions. It gives a comforting sense of carrying out the wishes of the dead, of being faithful to their last requests. If the services are planned according to the deceased's wishes, family and friends can truly say, "She would have wanted it this way."

But in some cases, following instructions may be neither practical nor comfortable. Your loved one may have specified that no services be held, while you and your family feel a strong need to gather in remembrance. Or the deceased may have instructed that her ashes be scattered in a way you can't condone. People may not feel comfortable playing the roles they have been instructed to play. Or the deceased may have requested an elaborate, expensive funeral that you simply cannot afford.

However, some instructions should be followed to the letter. For example, if a person has specified that the service be held according to a certain religious rite, we believe that wish should be carried out, even if the religion is unfamiliar or unappealing to you. But in many other, smaller respects, you needn't feel bound to follow instructions slavishly, particularly if they are in conflict with your own sense of propriety or your ability to carry them out.

WILL THE SERVICE BE RELIGIOUS OR SECULAR?

Choosing between a religious and a secular service is often easy. If the person was deeply religious or a longtime member of a certain congregation, of course it would be natural to hold a service of her denomination. But if the person was quite clearly nonreligious—an atheist, a skeptic, or simply someone who never had any contact with organized religion of any kind—it would seem quite inappropriate to hold a religious service.

Some choices are more difficult. Many people, while not actively religious, nonetheless want to return to the religion of their childhood for burial. Many families, too, want to take the opportunity to bring their loved one back, even posthumously, to the fold.

Consider both the wishes of the person who has died and the needs of family, friends, and the community. Is there anything about a religious service that would be jarring or inappropriate? Many of us can remember our discomfort at services in which the deceased's deep religious faith was extolled—a faith which everyone but the pastor knew had never existed in reality. On the other hand, it might be offensive or disappointing to others if a religious service were not held. If a person's religious convictions were tepid but it would mean a great deal to important family members and the community that a religious service be held, we think it is perfectly appropriate.

In most cases, the choice of a religious service will also govern the choice of location (a church, chapel, or synagogue), the celebrants (clergy), and the type of service (the rite of that denomination). Some churches are more flexible than others, but usually a religious service gives far less leeway for creative expression than does a secular service.

Choosing a secular service, of course, doesn't mean abandoning religion altogether. A secular service is simply one that is held outside a religious establishment and one that you, not the clergy, plan and conduct. There are many clergy who will happily participate in such a service if you wish to include a religious element. Conversely, there are some religions, Unitarianism for example, that permit services that are close to secular. (See Chapter 2, "Planning a Religious Service," for more details.)

WILL YOU HOLD A FUNERAL, A MEMORIAL SERVICE, OR BOTH?

Traditionally, there is only one distinction between a funeral and a memorial service: at a funeral the body is present; at a memorial service it is not. Thus, a memorial service is most likely to be held for someone who has been lost at sea or in a plane crash, for someone who was either cremated or died in a distant country, or for someone who for some reason was buried before relatives and friends could assemble. In all other ways, funerals and memorial services may be identical, and in many places and in many religions the ceremonies preferred at both are the same, or nearly so.

In practical terms, however, the two are very distinct and becoming more so. While the purpose of the funeral service hasn't changed much, the memorial service has come to serve a much broader function. People are increasingly turning to memorial services either to replace standard funeral services or to supplement them, because they are finding in them—or creating in them—a flexibility that enables them to serve many purposes.

The funeral remains the basic ceremony. It is usually held within a few days of death and consists of a series of three steps: a viewing or "wake"; a formal service; and a graveside rite. Formalities at the viewing and at the graveside rite are usually minimal.

Funerals and memorial services can be either religious or secular, though funerals are more likely to be religious. The biggest difference between them is one of mood and function. Because the funeral occurs with the body present, there is a greater emphasis on death, mourning, and the loss of the person. The atmosphere is usually somber and sad. The function of a memorial service, on the other hand, is to celebrate a person's life. The focus is on memories and recollections, and on his contributions to the lives of his friends, family, and community. Many memorial services are held later after death than funerals are, and the mood is likely to be more upbeat.

"A memorial service lets people honor the memory of the deceased," one rabbi said. "The important difference, I think, is that there has been such a psychological change among people. There is more emphasis at the time of death on the pain and grief of the family. Thirty days later, at a memorial service, people are at a different stage in the grieving process. Therefore, funerals and memorial services are different phenomena. Their mood, tenor, and nature are different thirty days later."

In the past, the funeral was not just the main service, it was usually the only service. These days, there are many possible combinations. Some people still hold only a formal funeral, with all memorializing and reminiscing done privately and informally. Some may choose to forgo a public funeral altogether, hold a small, private burial or cremation service, and then have a public memorial service later.

One common practice these days is to hold both a funeral and a memorial service. In this case, the funeral is often religious and the memorial service more secular. When Stephen Tudor, a professor at Wayne State University in Detroit, was lost in Lake Michigan during a sailing race, his brother, an Episcopal priest, celebrated one memorial service in a church. Some time later, his colleagues held a second service at the university.

Some religions, especially ones tied strongly to particular ethnic groups, already have an informal tradition of pairing a strictly religious service with a more informal secular service. The latter usually occurs within the context of an elaborate meal prepared by the congregation and served immediately after the religious service. Some variation on that format could also be useful for those who wish both a religious service and a secular one.

Here are some of the differences between funerals and memorial services, and the ways in which they can be used.

WHO HOLDS THE SERVICE?

Funerals are still largely planned and carried out by families or very close friends. Memorial services can be held by a wide variety of interested people. We have come upon memorial services held by colleagues, golf partners, high school classmates, and college roommates.

One of the reasons for the increasing popularity of memorial services is the diversity—both geographical and social—of the communities in which we live. A person may grow up in Kansas, go to school in Florida, and live in Minnesota, California, and Oregon, leaving behind friends and colleagues who will remember and care. When the funeral service is held too far away or too soon after the death to permit some group of people to gather, a separate memorial service is often held in another location. Memorial services thus give several different communities the opportunity to remember their colleagues, classmates, and friends.

Memorial services are even held by people who were in some way touched by the life of the person who died but are not close enough to the family to attend the funeral. For instance, although her funeral was in her home state of California, people in Cheyenne, Wyoming, held a memorial service for Jessica Dubroff, the seven-year-old pilot who crashed taking off from the city's airport.

WHO ATTENDS THE SERVICE?

Funeral services can be either small and private, attended by only the nearest family members and friends, or large and public, attended by anyone who cares to go. Memorial services offer another possibility. They may be planned and carried out by and for the benefit of a specific group of people. Therefore, they can sometimes take on a very particular tone as people who know one another well in a specific context can speak intimately about their relationship with the person who has died.

WHEN IS THE SERVICE HELD?

Because a funeral is usually closely associated with burial, it is most often held within several days of death. A memorial service offers greater flexibility. It can be held right after death, as a funeral is, or it can be delayed, even for quite a while.

Some cultures and religious traditions call for memorial services to be held on specific dates, for example, thirty days after death. Otherwise, the service may be delayed for several weeks or months to give people time to plan and to gather friends. Some very effective services are held on the one-year anniversary of death.

Many people, however, recommend that a memorial service not be delayed too long. They suggest that it is in the first few weeks after death that the loss is most deeply felt and a memorial service can do the most good. Later, when the reality of death has begun to sink in, it may be harder for those closest to the deceased to muster the emotional fortitude to create a meaningful service.

"I advise people to have the memorial service very soon after the death and funeral," said the Reverend Robert Lee, pastor of the First Congregational Church in Burlington, Vermont. "The reason is that the memorial service can be important in the grieving process. Death needs a public acknowledgment to set it in context. That's important. Survivors need to integrate death into their life."

If people delay the memorial service, said Dr. Tom Leland of Second-Ponce de Leon Baptist Church in Atlanta, "the death remains open-ended. They don't realize that they need to have a memorial service to deal with their own grief, to bring closure."

CHECKLIST FOR PLANNING A FUNERAL OR MEMORIAL SERVICE

____ Set aside time for planning.

____ Look for instructions from the deceased and follow them if possible. Even if you decide not to follow them to the letter, you want to have them and not discover them months later.

____ Get help. Be creative in seeking out those who can assist you.

____ Find a résumé and think about the places in which the deceased lived and worked and the activities she pursued.

____ Decide whether you want a religious or secular service:

- Do you want this service to be held completely within the confines of religious tradition?

- Do you want only some limited religious aspects?

- Would any aspect of a religious service be inappropriate?

- Do you prefer a completely secular service?

____ Think about how much control you want over the creation and execution of the service:

- Do you want to create a service completely on your own?

- Do you want to build on existing traditions?

- Do you prefer the comfort and security of well-known ceremonies?

____ Decide what level of formality you want:

- How formal was the deceased?

- How formal are you and the community around you?

____ Think about the different communities that will attend:

- Is one service sufficient?

- Are there other groups that may also want to hold services?

- Are there many people who are too far away to attend?

- Are there any time limitations?

- Would a religious service be more appropriate for one community and a secular service for another?

___ Consider the personality of the person who has died:

- Did she attend religious services regularly?

- What kind of life did she live?

- What was she known for? Her garden? Her hobbies? Her accomplishments? Her friendships? Her love of color? Her love of art? Her charitable work?

- Who were her close friends?

- What did she read?

- What music did she listen to?

___ Decide whether you want to hold a funeral, a memorial service, or both.

___ Decide who will hold the service.

___ Decide when it will be held.

___ Decide who will attend.

CHAPTER TWO

PLANNING
A RELIGIOUS SERVICE

The most common form of funeral and memorial service is religious. The vast majority of Americans identify themselves as members of some church or denomination. Those who don't nonetheless often express a desire to be buried and memorialized from a church. One woman facing death from cancer hadn't been to church in a long time. But when she expected she was going to die, she went to visit the local Catholic priest to introduce herself, "so that he wouldn't be burying a stranger." Families, too, often have a strong preference for holding a church service, even for someone whose religious affiliation during his lifetime was only modest.

Choosing a religious service often eases the process considerably. If the person who has died, his family, or his close friends were regular practitioners, there will be a built-in community to help support and guide you through the process. The formal rites associated with each major religion also provide a strong framework for the service.

The usual location for religious services is a church or synagogue. They can, however, also be held in a variety of other locations—the graveside at the time of interment, for example—either as the sole service or following a church service. But a religious service can present complications. For some people, it may be their first major contact with organized religion since, perhaps, their wedding or the baptism of their children. People returning to the religion of their childhood or to their family's traditional religion may find that much has changed since they were active members. Or they may find to their surprise that they have changed. The service you remember may no longer be appropriate for you, your family, or your deceased loved one.

Religions vary considerably in the rigor with which they prescribe a set service. Some hew rigidly to their canon and their liturgy, and variation from these traditions is scarcely permitted. Others at the opposite end of the spectrum seek simply to provide a general spiritual framework for what might otherwise be a strictly secular service.

While many people prefer to individualize their services, the weight of tradition is still extremely comforting. "People are grateful for ritual," said Yates Hafner, who helped with both a religious and a secular service for his good friend Stephen Tudor after his death during a sailing race. "You can't ad-lib a memorial service. It's fine to have forms which are beautiful. You needn't think and plan them out. You follow the form—the rhythm of life and ritual carries you through." The religious service with all its forms was "a salutary experience," he said. "It didn't seem mechanical."

The clergy of many religions offer services to anyone who requests them, but some will not perform a service for a deceased who was not a practicing member of their faith. It may take friends and family some time to find a receptive church. "I hear stories," said the Reverend Robert Lee. "The family said that a Christian minister wouldn't do it because the deceased wasn't a Christian and a Jewish rabbi wouldn't do it because the deceased wasn't Jewish."

Although much depends on the denomination, local traditions may also vary considerably. Even in very strict or very relaxed faiths, the individual personality and predilections of the local clergy can make a difference. Some clergy interpret the regulations of their denominations very precisely. Others have a more laissez-faire attitude. It's therefore very important both to understand the framework of the religious tradition you choose and to speak directly and clearly with the clergy who will officiate.

Failure to do this may result in some unpleasant surprises. One group of friends, counting on the liberal reputation of Episcopalians, planned a memorial service within that church, only to discover late in the process that the clergy wouldn't permit the loose format of unstructured eulogies that they had arranged. Other problems can arise when an ordained friend or relative is asked to officiate but local custom frowns on visiting clergy.

In many religious rites, the opportunity for family and friends to participate in or personalize the service is minimal. But even in the most restrictive of religions, there are some opportunities. For example, in denominations that restrict music to sacred selections, there can still be a great deal of leeway. And don't underestimate the power of familiar hymns to move and comfort. There is probably no song as moving as "Amazing Grace" or the old, traditional doxology: "Praise God from Whom All Blessings Flow." Other religions will permit selections from sacred classical music, which provides a huge selection of beautiful, dignified, moving pieces—everything from the familiar "I Know That My Redeemer Liveth" from Handel's *Messiah* and "Jesu, Joy of Man's Desiring" by Johann Sebastian Bach to grandiose selections such as requiems by Brahms and Mendelssohn and even funeral music by Wagner.

Some religious denominations also restrict eulogies, allowing only a few very brief remarks by family or close friends. In others, only the clergy is traditionally allowed to speak. If this is the case, it is advisable that, as part of your planning process, you sit down with the clergy and talk over in great detail what the deceased was like and what points you want emphasized. This is important whether your clergyman has been a family friend for decades or is someone you have just met. Share as much as possible of your knowledge of the deceased with the clergy. Even small errors can be upsetting to people. And you may also forestall bigger errors. The family and friends of Nina Weisse, for example, sat through a service during which the priest used the common pronunciation of her name—"Nee-na"—rather than the unusual pronunciation she actually used—"Nye-na."

How do you find clergy to conduct a service if you are not a member of a congregation yourself? One way, of course, is simply by calling around to denominations with which you are familiar. Funeral homes also keep lists of local clergy who are willing to officiate for people outside their congregations. Funeral and memorial service practices vary widely from denomination to denomination. The following descriptions are, in general, what you may expect to find.

EPISCOPAL

While Episcopalians tend to be socially liberal, they are extremely conservative in terms of liturgy and protective of their rites when those rites are held in their church.

The language of the Episcopal memorial and funeral service will be familiar to many. It is drawn from the Book of Common Prayer, the moving, cadenced, sonorous work from which the services of many other Protestant denominations are drawn. It offers the comfort of tradition and dignity.

It does not, however, allow for much personalizing. Most Episcopalian clergy require that existing traditions be followed closely and won't allow much variation in readings, music, or tributes. "Among Episcopalians there is an element of snobbishness surrounding the liturgy," said the Reverend Craig Bustrin, a priest at Saint Michael's Episcopal Church in New York. "The Book of Common Prayer has lent exalted language to the service for four hundred years. Music in the Anglican service has been of a high order of quality and professionalism. The service generally is done in high style. For many, to work a guitar song into the memorial service would be vulgar."

Thus, the vast majority of readings at Episcopal services are scriptural, though exceptions may be made for dignified classical or modern poetry such as works by Shakespeare, George Herbert, or W. H. Auden. Music, likewise, is restricted in most congregations. "We're not very flexible" on the issue of secular music in church, said Gary Gura, parish administrator of Saint Luke's in the Fields Episcopal Church in New York. "We don't permit the use of a tape recorder or a microphone. It's not a Broadway show."

It is true that in some parts of the country more adventurous Episcopalian clergy may — on their own — permit creative, offbeat services. (One Episcopal priest in New York, for example, presided over a service at which a ballerina in a lavender tutu pirouetted down the aisle. Big Bird delivered a eulogy at the funeral for puppeteer Jim Henson at the Cathedral of Saint John the Divine in New York. And in San Francisco, another Episcopal priest held a memorial service in a laundromat.) But in general, for services held inside the church, Episcopalians permit only the most modest of variations on the standard rites.

HOW CAN THE SERVICE BE PERSONALIZED?

A wide range of readings is permitted if they are mainly classical or otherwise determined to be "serious." Many congregations do allow family members or friends to speak but limit those speeches to a few minutes so they don't overwhelm the religious service. Many churches will allow a display of some important aspect of the work of the person who has died—photographs or art, for example. Many Episcopalians who want a more personalized service choose one of two routes: either they choose a mainly secular service at which they invite a member of the Episcopal clergy to speak, or they have a religious funeral ceremony, followed a few days or weeks later by a secular memorial service.

WHERE DOES THE SERVICE TAKE PLACE?

Episcopal services normally take place in an Episcopal church. Many clergy, however, can be quite helpful about advising those who want to create a service outside the church.

EASTERN ORTHODOX

Most Eastern Orthodox services are likewise very conservative and admit very little variation. The service is quite simple and usually quite short. The order of the service follows this basic format: an opening prayer, a hymn, a reading from the Scriptures, a homily, a hymn, and a closing prayer. It usually lasts less than thirty minutes.

The clergy consults with the bereaved to ask them about their preferences. But the service admits only the narrowest of possible variations— usually in the choice of Scripture readings. "A memorial service isn't simply allowing the bereaved to do whatever they like," said Vince Rossi, an Eastern Orthodox priest. "The event needs solemnity and mystery. There has to be an acknowledgment of sorrow, an acknowledgment that we're up against a mystery and have to come to terms with it. A lot of people don't have a clear understanding of what standards are in good religious taste. New prayers can be written, but they need to conform to the basic pattern and style of the existing service. The Orthodox faith doesn't put much of a premium on originality in its services."

HOW CAN THE SERVICE BE PERSONALIZED?

You can select Scripture readings as well as music, but the music must be either traditional hymns or drawn from the classical repertory. Eastern Orthodox religions also have a long tradition of informal memorial services, which tend to take place spontaneously during the elaborate meal that follows the funeral service. Those seeking a more personal, informal memorial may want to work within this two-part format.

WHERE DOES THE SERVICE TAKE PLACE?

The service takes place almost exclusively within an Orthodox church.

BAPTIST

Baptists don't, strictly speaking, have a formal liturgy like that of the Episcopalian, Catholic, or Eastern Orthodox religions. Each church follows its own customs, and there can be a wide variation in what is permitted. By and large, Baptists are, however, fairly conservative and a memorial service is a religious service. The variations that are allowed must take place strictly within a religious context.

Thus, most Baptist churches will allow contemporary music—even country and rock—as long as it is religious. They will also allow memorials and eulogies if they are short and serious and focus on the person's life in a religious context. And they will allow brief expositions of a person's work or art if they are in good taste. But the focus of the service is clearly on redemption and not on looking backward. "Baptists are mostly not preoccupied with the body or the condition of the body. Baptists are concerned with the condition of the soul—whether or not the soul is prepared to meet God," said Dr. Tom Leland, at Second-Ponce de Leon Baptist Church in Atlanta.

At their most conservative, Baptists turn away altogether from remembering a person's life. Dr. Joseph L. Roberts, the pastor of Ebenezer Baptist Church in Atlanta, the church of Dr. Martin Luther King, performs a religious funeral service based on the Episcopal Book of Common Prayer. Tributes or memorials to the dead person are held only during the church coffee hour.

To Dr. Roberts, no memorialization is appropriate in a religious service. "Life is a cycle," he said. "We came from our place with God, and we will go back to God. Our lives are not in our bodies. In my church, I wouldn't allow these sorts of memorial services that I see performed for people in Hollywood—where person after person talks about the deceased. I feel the proper place for that sort of thing is not in church but in the concert hall. You get the bereaved together at a memorial service and they all remember how he liked to drink beer. What's edifying about that? What's redemptive about that?"

The Baptist service consists of an invocation, the singing of hymns in which the congregation usually participates, readings from the Scriptures, and a eulogy, which is often delivered by the clergyman. Family and friends are sometimes allowed to speak.

HOW CAN THE SERVICE BE PERSONALIZED?

While Baptist services are quite strictly prescribed, they also admit variety within the format. The important role that traditional hymns play in the lives of Baptists means that there are many to choose from that will have strong meaning for family and friends. Eulogies that address the Christian character of the person who has died are permitted, and a simple but moving service can emerge from the heartfelt recollections of people who were close to the deceased.

WHERE IS THE SERVICE HELD?

The service can be held at a Baptist church or a funeral home.

ROMAN CATHOLIC

Roman Catholics, once among the most rigidly ceremonial of denominations, have become much more flexible in recent years. The basic Roman Catholic funeral mass remains formal, however. It is most often held in the church itself (although occasionally a mass may be held in a funeral home or in the home of the family or friends of the deceased). It is presided over by a priest in full vestments, and incense is usually burned. The underlying ceremony is the same as for a Catholic mass and consists of a profession of faith, a confession of sins, prayers for the departed, a consecration, and a Communion. The Catholic service includes three Scripture readings: one from the Old Testament, one from the Epistles, and one from the Gospels. A psalm can also be read. And there are usually four points at which there is music or singing: at the opening of the service, at the offertory, at Communion, and at closing.

In some communities there is a trend back to the traditional, conservative service. Some people even choose to have important parts of the service read in the Latin of the traditional Catholic mass. Because much about a Catholic service may be unfamiliar even in English, anyone expecting non-Catholics to attend may want to include a program with explanations.

Historically, at a Catholic service the eulogy has been delivered by the priest and music has been minimal. That has begun to change, however, and—depending on the preferences of the local clergy—it is much more possible to have friends and family speak, perform music, or read poetry. And while traditional hymns are still preferred at the main service, Catholics have also become very open to nontraditional music, allowing and even encouraging members of the congregation to perform.

HOW CAN THE SERVICE BE PERSONALIZED?

Outside the formal funeral mass, Catholics have now begun to allow, even encourage, many other possible services. If you choose not to have a formal funeral mass, you might have a more informal scriptural service. Catholics have also become much more flexible about holding informal services outside church—at a funeral home, at the place of burial, at another outdoor location, even at the home of the deceased or one of his friends.

Some Catholic organizations have even developed an informal alternative liturgy for memorial services. These services are religious in nature but are also highly participatory and symbolic. The set of "Commemoration Services for the Four Seasons" is an example. It includes services for spring, summer, fall, and winter, using events and symbols appropriate to each season. A winter service, therefore, would make use of Christmas carols; a spring service would include a planting. The Catholic wake—the period of visiting the body—has also traditionally been used as a time for people to share their stories and memories of the deceased.

WHERE IS THE SERVICE HELD?

A Catholic funeral mass is held in a Catholic church. In recent years, however, Catholic clergy have become very flexible about assisting at memorial services held in many different locations, such as funeral homes or the homes of friends or family.

PRESBYTERIAN

A Presbyterian service can be either very formal or very informal, depending on your preference and the preference of the clergy. Like the religions that have a formal liturgy, the Presbyterians offer an order for the service which consists of a Scripture reading, a prayer, a hymn, a psalm, another Scripture reading, the Lord's Prayer, and then a blessing.

Within that order, however, there is great flexibility. The Presbyterian liturgy is a suggestion, not a command. There is a strong stress on readings and music that are considered appropriate to church, but additions are also allowed. "First come the prayer and Scripture," said the Reverend Ted Wardlaw, pastor of Central Presbyterian Church in Atlanta. "Then, after that, it's all right for the family to read their selection from Kahlil Gibran."

Presbyterian pastors are also likely to be very helpful in arranging general meetings of remembrance. "I would approve of a service where you have a Christian community gathering," Mr. Wardlaw said. Liturgical and interpretive dance is permitted. So are poetry and singing. Still, the emphasis is strongly religious. "If you're not a member of the church, you could just as easily have the service in a recital hall or restaurant," Wardlaw added. "But what is profound, over time, is the irreducible minimum of a service. Our heritage overcomes other particulars."

HOW CAN THE SERVICE BE PERSONALIZED?

Discussions with clergy and with the family and friends of the deceased about their preferences and degree of participation will result in a more informal, personalized service. The service will be led by clergy, but it can be expanded to eulogies and remembrances as well as poetry and music.

WHERE IS THE SERVICE HELD?

Presbyterian funeral services are held in the church. However, Presbyterian clergy are usually very flexible about assisting at services in a wide range of nontraditional locations.

METHODIST

The Methodist service is among the most flexible of the Christian services. Its basic format includes an Old Testament lesson, the reading of two or three psalms, a lesson from the Epistles or Revelation, and a Gospel reading. But the actual service depends completely on the wishes and preferences of the family and the individual pastor. Families and friends are encouraged to be actively involved in the creation of a service and participate in it. The family can request music or have no music. There can be speakers or no speakers. Because of its flexibility, the Methodist church service usually serves as a memorial service as well.

UNITARIAN

In general, Unitarian services are focused on life, humanity, and relationships. "The service is very this-worldly," said John Weston, who heads All Souls Unitarian Universalist Church in Kansas City, Missouri. "Unitarian Universalists are as liberal as you can get and still be a church."

Unitarian services vary across the country. Unlike many other denominations, Unitarians have very little in the way of central authority, regarding the churches themselves as the primary units. In general, the services have no set format and use no Scripture. Instead, they depend on poetry, music, and eulogies.

"There is a big difference between a sacramental service, which is essential to salvation—like those held by Episcopalians, Lutherans, Roman Catholics," Weston said. "In more liberal denominations, the service becomes more expressionistic. We speak of the dead, his or her relationships, what they savored, and what they missed."

Weston holds a more formal service and selects poetry in consultation with the family. "We use poems that allow them to go through the steps of grieving and gain some acceptance for their own position vis-à-vis the death," he said. Some kind of live music is performed, he delivers the eulogy, and then other people make public reminiscences.

JEWISH

Each of the three mainstream Jewish sects—Orthodox, Conservative, and Reform—has its own rules for memorial services. The Orthodox are, of course, the most conservative and formal in their adherence to ritual and the Reform the most liberal.

Funerals among the three major Jewish sects also differ linguistically. The Orthodox service uses more Hebrew; the Conservative about half Hebrew; the Reform no Hebrew except for the saying of the Kaddish. The underlying format, however, is the same. There are scriptural readings and eulogies by the family of the deceased—or, if not by them, by the rabbi. The traditional prayer of death is the Kaddish, which is spoken only by the immediate family of the deceased. The Kaddish differs from a rabbi's traditional liturgical prayer recited at a funeral.

Whichever type of Judaism people practice, American Jews all have the tradition of going to the home of the deceased after the funeral. The traditional period of deep mourning—seven days—is called "shiva." And while the family sits shiva, everyone is invited to the home of the deceased to offer condolences. In many congregations part of the evening service is celebrated at the house. Generally, in more conservative congregations, it is only the closest family friends who come during the first day of shiva.

The Jewish belief in an afterlife is different from that of Christianity. If the deceased has had a long life and accomplished many things, this is reason for celebration. But there is no concept of a joyful afterlife. "For Jews, death is somber. We are not a faith that celebrates death with dancing and drinking over the deceased's departure to heaven," said one rabbi.

HOW CAN THE SERVICE BE PERSONALIZED?

There are practically no opportunities to personalize an Orthodox service. With Reform congregations, it is up to the individual rabbi. Some rabbis will permit song, music, even dance at a memorial service. Still others prefer to leave such variations to a service or memorial that is held thirty days after the death.

WHERE IS THE SERVICE HELD?

The more traditional the congregation, the more likely the service will be held in a synagogue. More liberal congregations and families hold services in funeral homes as well as other locations.

CHECKLIST FOR PLANNING
A RELIGIOUS SERVICE

____ What are the local customs of the denomination you prefer?

- What are the personal preferences of the priest, minister, or rabbi?

- What type of music will be allowed? Some denominations allow only specific hymns. Some allow religious classical music. Some put restrictions on the types of instruments allowed or who can sing. Some allow singing by the congregation but not by soloists. Some do not allow recorded music.

- What readings, if any, will be allowed? Some allow only Scripture. Some allow dignified classical readings. Be especially clear about your choice if you want something unusual.

- Who will be allowed to speak at the service?

- What variations—additions or subtractions—will be allowed from the denomination's own service?

- Will any other clergy be welcome to officiate?

- Does the denomination have any restrictions on performing ceremonies for someone who is not an active practitioner of that faith?

—— If a priest, minister, or rabbi will deliver the eulogy, make sure he or she knows as much as possible about the deceased (some clergy will take the initiative; some may not). Also make sure he or she:

- Pronounces the deceased's name correctly.

- Knows about the deceased's personal preferences.

- Knows any particular family circumstances that are important.

- Knows important personal facts about the deceased.

- Knows telling anecdotes that will make the eulogy personal.

—— If the memorial service will be in a denomination that is not familiar to many of the people who will be attending, be sure to include detailed instructions in the program (see Chapter 10).

—— If you are looking for more flexibility:

- Try a Unitarian or Methodist church.

- Hold a religious funeral followed by a secular memorial service.

- Consider a service held in a funeral home with a priest, minister, or rabbi officiating.

- Consider a secular service held outside a church at which a priest, minister, or rabbi is asked to speak or provide a blessing.

CHAPTER THREE

MEMORABLE
RELIGIOUS SERVICES

A BAPTIST SERVICE FOR A GENEROUS WOMAN

Mildred Lee was a well-known figure in Atlanta. She and her husband had owned many bars and nightclubs around the city. Her memorial service was held at Virginia Highland Baptist Church in downtown Atlanta. The service was religious in form, with organ music and hymns sung by the congregation. It was also religious in content, as each speaker gave moving testimony to the way Mrs. Lee had put her religious faith into practice.

The service opened with an organist playing Baptist hymns, a reading from Isaiah, and a prayer. The congregation sang "Near to the Heart of God" and "Amazing Grace." Then Mrs. Lee's children and grandchildren and the children she had raised rose to speak:

*

"I'm her grandson. I loved my grandma very much. If I'd known she was in trouble, I would have helped her. There was no finer woman. She said, 'Be strong.' I loved Grandma and Grandfather. I know she's happy now with him. She was a fine lady to me and to everyone else. I'll always remember her."

*

"I'm [his] brother. I wrote down some things I want to say. She touched each of our lives. I'll be brief. I told my roommate this morning what I felt about her passing away. It probably won't completely hit me until some days from now. She was the closest this family will make to an angel. I feel she was an angel. A saint. She brought me to Christ, to prayer. No mumbo jumbo. She'll be watching me, keeping me on the spiritual track. She helped me. Through the good she did she showed me how. I see God's greatness through her. She's watching over me. I remember how close to God she was. I wrote the same thing to my roommate. I went to her apartment. There were her most treasured things on the wall. There were angels she had made hanging on the wall, and pictures of Jesus. She taught me Jesus through her actions. She knew we'd be facing challenges in life. I'll miss her guidance, but I also know that she's in a better place.

"She gave to people that others don't give to. She was with people that others wouldn't be with. She loved people that others wouldn't love. It recalls the words—love is kind, love doesn't envy, boast, or be proud, be angry. She never failed us."

*

"She was my mother from age sixteen on. I'm now fifty. She's the only person I ever respected. She's here and she's in heaven. She didn't have much in a financial way to leave to people she loved. She had already given it away. It's in our hearts and minds. She left us a legacy. In the future she'll make the way clear. She always did."

*

"She touched me deeply. When I heard she died, it made me think. A lot of people were raised in her house. She fed us, clothed us, took us to church. I can't express my grief. I haven't been in this church for twenty years. When I came here today, it all came back to me."

*

"I'm another one she took in. She was our mom. I have a lot of memories of her reading the Bible to us before we'd walk to school."

*

"I'm another 'kid.' I never had any mother but her. I put her through a lot, as some of you know, but she never gave up. I love all of you for coming here. I know she would be happy to see us all here together."

*

Then the minister read a brief eulogy: "Our lives are short and precious. The Scriptures tell us to number our days. We only have one life. What are we to do with it? She embodied the word 'Christian.' She was a follower of Jesus Christ. He told us to suffer the little children. He loved the disenfranchised in their communities. She did also. They say she had no money at her death, she had given it all away. She could have used the money to be buried well. But she knew what was valuable in life and put her money there instead.

"We don't take people that we don't know into our homes. I don't. It's not a trusting society. There is a lot of fear out there. She saw through that. Jesus Christ said, 'Do unto the least of these.' She did. She took it seriously.

"She also sang well. She sang here for us. A lot of you were brought to Christ here through her.

"A woman telephoned who wasn't able to come here this afternoon. The woman said that of the many things that Mildred did for her, bringing her to Christ was the most important. . . .

"Mary and Martha were troubled at the death of their brother, Lazarus. He was not only their brother, he was also their provider. They knew of Jesus' powers. They felt if Jesus had come in time he could have saved Lazarus. We all know what happened, how Jesus called him from the grave. He called upon all 'those who believe in me, rise up.' Mildred knew this. We celebrate her life and the many things she accomplished. But we're also celebrating the resurrection because we are made whole in Christ. Death has no sting. It's only a sting for the rest of us. Mildred is in a place where there is great joy and no suffering.

"Mildred was a good example of salt and light—a good example for us to follow."

It was a memorial service rather than a funeral, because there was no body present. Mrs. Lee had donated her body to Emory University's medical school.

TWO MEMORIAL SERVICES FOR A LOST SAILOR

No funeral was held for Stephen Tudor, a professor at Wayne State University in Detroit. He had been sailing in a race on Lake Huron and had not returned. His boat was found drifting; his safety harness had snapped. After he had been missing for three or four weeks, his family decided to hold his service.

There were two memorial services for Dr. Tudor, both of which were held in churches. The first service, held at Christ Church in Grosse Pointe, was religious. The second was secular, held at Saint Andrew's Hall, a refurbished church at Wayne State University that is used for lectures, concerts, and recitals. It had stained-glass windows and was light and airy.

The religious service was organized and celebrated by Dr. Tudor's brother, an Episcopal priest. The secular service was organized by a longtime colleague at Wayne State, Dr. Yates Hafner. Each service was very different. The first had music and Scripture; the second had none.

"The first . . . had an aura of religion," said Dr. Hafner, who was involved in both services. "It was sorrowful, and there were tears shed. The second was more open, more sunshiney. It was looser and had spontaneity. Its tone was lighter, and people felt freer to tell funny stories." But, he added, "both services had a strong therapeutic value to family and friends."

The majority of the first service was a standard Episcopalian service, drawn from the Book of Common Prayer. Steve's wife, Ellie Tudor, determined some of the elements: She picked which Scriptures were to be read (Psalm 139) and what music would be played (selections from Handel's *Messiah*, as well as Welsh songs to honor Dr. Tudor's Welsh heritage; Dr. Tudor's son, Michael, also played classical guitar). Dr. Tudor had been a poet, so Mrs. Tudor also selected several of his most recent poems to be read. One was "Haul-Out," a poem he had written about putting his boat away for the season:

> *It's only my life, this banged up, obsolete*
> *plastic heap with its faded gelcoat, frayed lines*

and . . . poor me. And we'd engaged so intensely,
skin, hair, teeth, nails, the roots of the flesh.
It barely seemed I'd the strength to make it to
Bristol, and now it's come time for hanging it up,
tanks cleared, engine drained, compartments
left open to air, and then the canvas
to tent us against the impossible weather.

At the Wayne State University memorial service there were no Scriptures or music. The poems of Dr. Tudor that were read at the Christ Church memorial service were also read at the Wayne State service. Anyone who wanted to speak was allowed to. Dr. Hafner and Mrs. Tudor contacted about a dozen people and arranged for them to speak. Another five or six rose spontaneously during the service.

Because he knew there would be many speakers, Dr. Hafner went to some care to arrange them in order: "I knew the people, therefore I knew their style and what they would say, which would tell amusing anecdotes and which would draw laughs and which would draw tears, and I interspersed them."

The length of time varied from person to person, but on average people spoke for five to ten minutes each about their association with Dr. Tudor and their feelings about him. They read his poetry as well as poems they had written since his disappearance. The service lasted two hours, and at the end his son, Michael, spoke. He thanked people for attending and made some personal remarks about his father.

A SIMPLE PRESBYTERIAN SERVICE FOR A LONGTIME MEMBER OF THE CONGREGATION

J. Alex Fife was a longtime member of the Columbia Presbyterian Church in Atlanta, sang in the choir, and regularly went to choir retreats and camps. That choir sang traditional hymns such as "Joyful, Joyful, We Adore Thee" and "A Mighty Fortress Is Our God" at his service, which was held in the church sanctuary.

The major speaker was the man who had been choir director for fifteen years and who had known Mr. Fife well. He spoke of Mr. Fife's love of trains and how he had known the names and schedules of famous trains. The only other speaker was a girl of thirteen, who read a eulogy her mother had written. It was about how she had first made the acquaintance of Mr. Fife when his daughter had worked as a baby-sitter for her family and how the girl had become a godsend to the family. But she recalled that his greatest gift was that he shared with her the importance of the church in his life. The whole service took about forty-five minutes, after which everyone returned to the church for a luncheon that had been prepared by about fifteen women in the congregation.

A WOMAN WHO PLANNED EVERYTHING

Cora Corn carried a sealed envelope in her purse and told her relatives not to open it until she died. When she did die, at eighty-nine years old, her daughter opened it and discovered a complete plan for her funeral. Mrs. Corn had picked the scriptural passage she wanted read: "Who can find a virtuous woman? For her price is far above rubies." She had picked the songs she wanted sung. (In the envelope were pages torn from a songbook, so there would be no mistake.) She had picked the young woman from the congregation she wanted to sing for her. And she had selected two ministers from the Baptist church to which she belonged, one to conduct the service and the other to read a prayer.

Most important for her family, Mrs. Corn had picked the pallbearers. "Each one was a special person to her," said her daughter, Edith Lee. Her nine children found the instructions extremely helpful. "She had every bit written down, and we did it exactly like she wanted it," said Mrs. Lee. Indeed, the family would have done things differently had it not been for those instructions: "We probably would have picked her grandsons for pallbearers," said Mrs. Lee. So they were glad to know her final wishes. Mrs. Corn had thought of even the smallest detail. In the envelope was a folded handkerchief with which she wanted her gnarled, arthritic hands covered.

CHAPTER FOUR

PLANNING A FORMAL, SECULAR SERVICE

Why hold a funeral or a memorial service in some place other than a church or a synagogue? One reason, of course, is that the person who has died had no religious beliefs or ties. It would seem inappropriate to seek out a religious service for an atheist or agnostic, or someone for whom religion had simply held no meaning. Sometimes, too, even a person who has practiced a religion may express a strong preference to be buried and memorialized without the ceremony of that church. Or a church may not perform a rite if, for example, its services are reserved for active, practicing members of that faith or that congregation.

But there are many other reasons to hold a secular service beyond the absence of religion. Some people simply want to hold a more flexible, personalized service without the restrictions a church might impose. Some may prefer a more relaxed, informal location than they feel a church might provide. Or a secular service may be more appropriate for the largely secular community in which the deceased lived.

Some may wish a military service that would take place outside church. There are also some fraternal organizations, such as the Masons, whose traditions include formal funeral and memorial services. And then there are people whose philosophy of life might be considered more humanist than religious. They, and the people around them, may wish a service that incorporates religious or moral values and symbolism but not an actual religious service.

What is a secular service? The possibilities are endless, since once you have decided to hold a service yourself, there are no external restrictions. You can say anything you like, read anything you like, play any music you like. The service can be as long or short as you want it to be. It can be held anywhere you choose, and you can invite anyone you like.

Even within all this freedom, however, some basic distinctions emerge. Memorial services held outside churches generally fall into two categories: formal and informal. An informal service is marked by spontaneity. It may be a service at which people are encouraged to speak freely without any order or planning. The seating may be informal. There may be shared activities and even ceremonies, but the formal underlying structure of such a service is minimal. Because the power of these services derives from shared memories and experiences, they work most effectively among groups of friends, colleagues, or acquaintances who have memories and experiences in common.

Formal services are not necessarily fancy or expensive. They are, rather, services that are held in a relatively formal location, with a formal structure. The choice between a formal and an informal service depends quite a bit on the personality of the person you are memorializing. There are some people who, in life, would have scoffed at the idea of a formal service with music, speeches, and pomp. For people who lived in jeans, scorned tradition, and loved iconoclasm, even the most tastefully done of formal services will still somehow seem inappropriate. But there are many other circumstances in which a formal service is the most appropriate, and not just for people whose personalities were formal. If informal services tend to work best with groups of friends who share common backgrounds or experiences, a more formal service can better serve to unify people who come from different backgrounds.

WHEN SHOULD IT BE HELD?

If a secular memorial service takes the place of the funeral service, it should naturally be held during the time period in which a funeral service would normally be held; that is, within several days to a week after the death. If the service is in addition to the funeral, there is more leeway. Some services are held on important anniversaries, for example, on a birthday, on Mother's Day, or on the one-year anniversary of death. Such services not only memorialize the person but also make reference to the importance of that day and to how the family and friends are carrying on with their lives in the absence of the person who has died.

But because an important function of memorial services is to help people through a difficult transition, they may also be held very close to the time of death. A common practice is to hold a funeral very soon after death, followed by a memorial service a week or ten days later. Such a timetable proves most helpful to family, friends, and community and also seems to best tap into the energies and emotions of the period immediately following the death.

WHERE SHOULD IT BE HELD?

People often turn to funeral homes to provide space for both funerals and memorial services. If a family is arranging the details of the funeral and burial through a funeral home, using the facilities of the home for the service offers the advantage of convenience. These facilities are, of course, set up with funerals and memorial services in mind. The size of the room and the seating can be adapted to the size of your group. The setting is appropriately sober, and logistical services, such as greeters, parking, a guest book, seating, and flowers can be provided. The home can also assist with placing obituaries and handling phone calls verifying the time, date, and place of the service. And of course, a funeral home is appropriate for a service in which the body or other remains will be present.

But people who wish to hold a truly personal memorial service may want to shy away from funeral homes. For one thing, their services come at a price. Each convenience is bought and, as many writers from Jessica Mitford on have noted, the recently bereaved are not always the most effective negotiators. More important for many people, however, is the desire to avoid the bland, impersonal feel of many funeral homes. They would prefer the beauty of a particular location, perhaps one overlooking the mountains or the sea or one that had some special meaning for the deceased or the family.

A formal service should be held in a place where comfortable seating can easily be arranged to accommodate the expected number of people. It should be quiet enough for guests to feel a sense of contemplation and also, of course, to hear the speakers. Ample parking and convenient access should be available. The location should also be able to provide a lectern for speakers and, if the service is to be a large one, a public-address system appropriate to the size of the room.

Just about any facility that is used to hold meetings could be a candidate. In small towns, local women's clubs often have attractive meeting places. Local art museums and conservatories often have public spaces that can be rented for functions. Historical societies often have public spaces that can be used for a memorial service for someone with strong ties to the region or to the town's history. Don't overlook colleges and universities. They often have nondenominational chapels or faculty clubs that can be used for services even for people who aren't associated with the institution. In big cities, alumni associations of bigger colleges sometimes have attractive meeting places that would be appropriate.

Places that usually specialize in weddings can also be very suitable for memorial services. Because they are often very beautiful or scenic—and are most often used for happy occasions—many people are coming to find that they can be a cheerful venue for a service that they are creating to celebrate the life of a person they loved. Such places include country clubs, large formal restaurants, hotel ballrooms, and meeting facilities in scenic locations.

Formal services can also be held in conjunction with burial, either of a body or of ashes. These graveside burial services are often very simple and—because participants usually stand—very short. If you choose to hold a graveside service, be sure that participants know the way to the grave site, providing them with a map if necessary. Also be sure to warn women to wear low-heeled shoes, since the uneven terrain of cemeteries can make walking difficult. And weather is always a factor. Also be aware that the presence of the coffin or ashes and the finality of burial can make this kind of service emotionally intense.

HOW LONG SHOULD IT LAST?

Family and friends should not let a memorial service run too long. If there are too many speakers, a service can drag on and become repetitive. The honor of speaking at the service should be reserved for those closest to the person who has died. And remember that the service is for the benefit of the entire community, not just of the individuals who speak. Music should be selected both for its moving qualities and for its place in the entire service. A memorial service—even one structured as a concert—is not actually a concert, and people should not be expected to sit through lengthy musical selections or endless readings.

The best length is between forty-five minutes and one hour. Services shorter than that may seem to be hurried or unfinished, and people may leave feeling "Was that all?" Longer than that, and people may begin to get restless and ready to leave.

WHO OFFICIATES?

Memorial services, both informal and formal, can proceed quite well without a central figure to officiate and direct them. If the service has been well ordered in advance, and if all participants are familiar with its structure and the timing of their roles, the service can move smoothly from one element to the next. But just as a religious service benefits from the presence of clergy to focus the attention of those gathered, so, too, do services outside the church benefit from someone to officiate.

The person who officiates should be someone who is both close to the family and sufficiently composed to handle the wide range of emotions a memorial service may elicit. He or she should take on the role of master of ceremonies, delivering the opening and closing remarks, explaining the significance of the music or readings, and introducing other speakers. Ideally, the person should also be gifted enough in public speaking to be able to handle the responsibility of a service before a large number of people. The presentation shouldn't be so practiced, however, that it leaves the impression that the service is a theatrical production rather than an intimate and genuine memorial. If a service outside the church is nonetheless intended to have a religious character, a priest or minister may informally officiate.

WHAT SHOULD ITS STRUCTURE BE?

Back in the 1960s, marriage ceremonies burst free from the rigid confines of church weddings, and brides and grooms began to be married in scenic outdoor locations. Demure lace and morning coats gave way to Indian cotton and bare feet. Seeking a more personal expression of their vows, couples wrote wedding services incorporating their own poetry, their friends' music, and speeches by family and friends. While more creative, many such services suffered one basic lack: liberated from tradition, they lacked a sense of moment. They were interesting and fun, but they did not seem to be very weighty or profound.

Memorial services, even more than weddings, require this sense of solemnity and importance. Those who perform religious services argue correctly that their formal structure provides a rhythm and tradition that are comforting in themselves. Too often, a memorial service planned outside a church appears to be nothing more than a series of speeches or an awkward fusing of music and meeting.

One way around that is to use a structure similar to that of a religious service. A formal structure—with a person to officiate and take the place of the minister and a clear-cut format to take the place of the liturgy—can give a sense of dignity to a service. There are many possible options. A basic structure would incorporate entrance music, a welcome, a statement of purpose, eulogies and possibly a brief ceremony, music, prayer and readings, and a summation and closing. Here are the elements that can be combined into a formal memorial service:

- *Entrance music:* Played as people assemble, entrance music will not be the centerpiece of the service and should not call attention to itself. It will, however, set the tone for the service, so it should be in keeping with your intent for the rest of the service. (See Chapter 13 for suggestions on what to play.)
- *Welcome:* To open the service, the welcome might begin: "We are

gathered here today to remember _____ , who died last week at the age of _____ after a long illness." It can be followed by a brief biography, which is especially desirable if people in attendance are from many different backgrounds or knew the deceased in a number of different contexts.

• *Statement of purpose*: Remarks summing up the attitude of the family and friends toward the service can be included in a statement of purpose. For a secular service that nonetheless has a religious content, it may also include a statement of religious belief. If that is not appropriate, you might state your belief that death is a stage of life and remind those in attendance of the continuity of life around them. In other, more purely secular services, you may want to make a brief statement about the contributions the person made during his lifetime and how much he will be missed by those who loved him.

• *Eulogy*: A brief speech delivered by someone close to the person who died, a eulogy is a personal remembrance of the deceased, praising his characteristics and contributions. (See Chapter 8 for a fuller discussion of eulogies.)

• *Music*: Musical interludes can be included. They are an opportunity to break up the intensity of the rest of the service and to add moments of reflection. They are also an opportunity to remember further the deceased by choosing music that is particularly apt. (See Chapter 13 for suggestions for appropriate music.)

• *Readings*: In religious services, readings from Scripture play a large role. In secular services, the choice of readings provides another opportunity to say something special and appropriate about either the person who has died or the grief his leaving will cause. It also offers those friends and family members who may not feel composed enough or sure enough of their speaking skills to deliver a eulogy an opportunity to participate in the service. (Chapter 11 provides suggestions for readings.)

• *Ceremony*: A short ceremony may be included within a memorial service. A candlelighting ceremony or the sharing of bread may invite audience participation. (Chapter 6 gives examples of ceremonies.)

• *Prayer*: Even many secular services—especially ones at which clergy officiate—can include prayers, blessings, and scriptural readings.

• *Responsive readings*: A memorial service may also include responsive readings. In a secular service, as in a church, these might consist of psalms or some other Scriptures read antiphonally—that is, one line read by the person officiating, the next read in unison by those in attendance. For example:

> *Officiant*: The Lord giveth, and the Lord taketh away.
> *People*: Blessed be the name of the Lord.

Other selections may also be chosen to be read in this manner. However, they must be chosen carefully for their gravity, rhythm, and balance. Alternatively, you can create your own responsive reading. (Chapter 6 offers some suggestions.)

• *Summation and closing*: Without a greeting and statement of purpose, the service can seem formless; without a summation and closing, it may seem too abrupt and unfinished. The officiant or a family member offers a final prayer or blessing, if appropriate, and then thanks everyone for coming and participating in the service. Exit music may also be played.

TYPICAL SERVICES

Here are some sample orders of services combining the various elements described above.

A SERVICE
WITH SEVERAL EULOGIES

Entrance music
Welcome and statement
 of purpose
Eulogy
Eulogy
Music
Eulogy
Music
Summation and closing
Exit music

A SERVICE
WITH A CEREMONY

Entrance music
Reading
Welcome
Music
Eulogy
Ceremony
Music
Summation and closing
Exit music

A SERVICE WITH PRAYER	A SERVICE WITH READINGS
Entrance music	Welcome
Reading	Responsive reading
Welcome	Reading
Prayer	Eulogy
Scripture reading	Music
Eulogy	Reading
Music	Responsive reading
Ceremony	Closing
Music	
Prayer	
Blessing and closing	

SPECIAL SERVICES

Formal services can also be created around special circumstances. For example, if the person who has died was especially noted in some field, a memorial service may be built around those accomplishments. For a musician, in particular, a very moving service can be built around the music that person wrote or performed. Such a service would follow the kind of formal structure noted above. However, the music, rather than being merely a background or an accompaniment, becomes the focus of the service.

Similarly, a writer might be remembered at a service in which the reading of excerpts from her works is central. An actress might be remembered at a service in which her best or her favorite roles are briefly reprised. Political activists may be remembered by recounting their achievements or through exhortations to complete a job left undone.

Such formal, public services which include readings or music are quite distinct from informal services, in which the readings or music become the centerpiece of the service. Jam sessions, jazz memorials, poetry readings—all these are examples of more informal kinds of services in which the art and the person's accomplishments take center stage.

CHECKLIST FOR PLANNING
A FORMAL, SECULAR SERVICE

_____ When should it be held?

_____ Where should it be held?

_____ How long should it last?

_____ Who will officiate?

- Clergy?

- Friend?

- Family member?

_____ Who will participate?

_____ What will the service include?

- Readings?

- Music?

- Scripture?

- Eulogies?

- Prayer?

- Some invented ritual?

- Some creative element?

_____ What should its structure be?

CHAPTER FIVE

MEMORABLE FORMAL, SECULAR SERVICES

AN UPBEAT SERVICE IN THE FACE OF TRAGEDY

Deborah Lewine had been dreading the call for years. Her brother, Jeff Haynes, had suffered from depression most of his life. In helping plan his memorial service after he committed suicide, Mrs. Lewine wanted to try to explain not just his death but his life as well. "We went to a funeral parlor," she said. "It would have been easy to let them take over. But we were turned off by the idea and wanted to do the service ourselves."

She and her sister-in-law found an unlikely place that turned out to be perfect. A man on Mr. Haynes's baseball team had a connection to a banquet facility. "The place was used for weddings and by vacationers," Mrs. Lewine said. "It overlooked the hills. It was great."

Mrs. Lewine went through her brother's own record collection to select the music. "Johnny Cash had recorded some old religious songs, and Jeff liked Johnny Cash," she said. "Some were amusing—'On your knees, you're taller than trees'—but some were good, upbeat country-and-western songs. The Mills Brothers had also made an album of hymns. We used Jeff's records. It set the tone—thinking about Jeff."

A minister who had been an acquaintance of Mr. Haynes and his wife conducted the service. He introduced everyone and led a prayer. But most of the service was "funny, wonderful stories that Jeff's friends told about him," said Mrs. Lewine. "There was a lot of laughter. There was a lot of talk."

Mrs. Lewine led the group in singing "Amazing Grace." Mrs. Haynes's brother sang "The Old, Rugged Cross." The softball team had put together a lunch, and everyone ate and shared reminiscences. Half of Mr. Haynes's ashes were scattered over San Francisco Bay.

Mrs. Lewine said that the service illustrated the differences in emotions between the time right after death and later, when the finality of it has sunk in. The first service was held a week after Mr. Haynes's death, and she said she had been "horribly upbeat" during most of the week — and the service was upbeat. A year later, when the other half of Mr. Haynes's ashes were buried in upper Michigan near the family's long-time vacation home, she, her children, and her father sang "Will the Circle Be Unbroken?" and "'Tis a Gift to Be Simple." That service was "much more somber," Mrs. Lewine said.

A CONCERT FOR A MAN OF MUSIC

Christopher Keene, the music director of the New York City Opera, continued to conduct even after he was so ill that he had to direct sitting down. His last concert was a matinee of the first professional American production of Paul Hindemith's opera *Mathis der Maler.**

After he died, a group made up of his family, his friends, and members of the opera company picked seven people to speak at his memorial service, which was held in a large concert hall in New York City. They spoke about Mr. Keene as a friend, a coworker, a parent, and a conductor. "A memorial service is a celebration of life," said Susan Wozel, a spokeswoman for the opera. "There was humor in the stories people told. After all, he was a funny man." But the bulk of the service, which lasted an hour and ten minutes, was a concert. The New York City Opera Company orchestra performed a piece Mr. Keene had recorded earlier with the Syracuse Symphony, the third movement from the Fifth

*See Peter Goodman, "Keene's Way," *Newsday*, October 9, 1995, p. B-3.

Symphony of Ralph Vaughn Williams. "It was what he wanted. His death wasn't sudden. He discussed his service with his family beforehand," said Ms. Wozel.

The orchestra also performed a selection from *Mathis der Maler*. More than a thousand people attended. "It was huge and well done," said Ms. Wozel. "I'd call it a service which was loving, personal, and professional."

A FUNNY SERVICE FOR A FUNNY MAN

"I asked them to be upbeat—or I'd take the microphone away from them," said Caroline Tolleson. The five family friends who spoke at the memorial service for her husband, Tom Tolleson, heeded her advice. "All of it was funny, and it left the people who attended laughing," she said.

It was only right. For Tom Tolleson had been a very funny man, always ready with a gag or a practical joke. He had delighted in trying to convince a stranger he was someone he was not. The more outrageous the story, the better.

The service was held at a funeral home in Atlanta with more than seven hundred people in attendance. It opened with a trumpet solo played by Mrs. Tolleson's cousin Herb Kraft, who is a well-known jazz trumpeter. A minister, Chick Thorington, a longtime friend of the Tolleson family, gave an invocation: "Gentle Father, God of love, with saddened hearts we come to you this morning that in worshiping You we may see both life and death in proper perspective and discover again how our darkness is dissipated in Your light." Then he read the Ninetieth Psalm: "The years of our life are three score and ten, or even by reason of strength, four score; yet their span is but toil and trouble, and they are soon gone and we fly away. So teach us to number our days that we may get a heart of wisdom."

Mr. Tolleson had had many friends stretching back for decades. Seven people spoke at the service, including a college roommate, a neighbor, and a son and a daughter. Nearly everyone spoke of his habit of putting people on—for example, by claiming to have been places and done things that he couldn't possibly have. "I found something that is absolutely astounding," said one man, his former roommate. "I looked at his driver's license, and he was born, according to the license, in 1929. And to think of a twelve-year-old boy fighting the vicissitudes of World War Two—it's unbelievable!"

"Tom's wit permeates this room," another man said. Then he told about the time Tom had introduced himself at a party as a test pilot for an experimental jet. He remembered Mr. Tolleson's liberal interpretation of his own age: "I used to say, 'Tom, you're the only person I've ever known who at one time was older than me. Later, somehow, I caught you, and even after that I passed you.' But Tom, dear soul, you win it all. We still don't know how old you are."

Mr. Tolleson had been full of life. Person after person rose to talk about football games, exuberant dinners, lunches they called "High Noon," vigorous tennis matches. Said one of his sons, "You can always measure a man's character by his friends. And that is certainly true in the case of my father. He had some great friends. And these gentlemen who testified about his life I think underline that point about him. Dad did indeed live a full life. And he lived it on his own terms. He even died on his own terms. If he had been able to script his death, this is the way he would have wanted to go."

The minister concluded with a prayer: "As you all have said, Tom Tolleson had the last word on a lot of things in life. But now today his death reminds us of the biblical truth that we do not have the last word on ourselves. As we live, though we may be strong in body, mind, and spirit, the ultimate word does not belong to us. But also it does not belong to death. It belongs to God alone. And that word, of which we can be certain, is in the end the word of grace." As guests left the service, an organist played "The Army Air Force Anthem," "Dixie," "Glory, Glory to Old Georgia," and "Amazing Grace."

CHAPTER SIX

PLANNING AN INFORMAL, CREATIVE SERVICE

What if a formal service just doesn't seem right? Or if a funeral home, banquet hall, or faculty club seems too stuffy? What if eulogies, readings, and songs aren't enough to express the feelings of family and friends? What if you want to be more creative?

Sometimes the personality of the deceased, or the character of her community, cries out for an informal, creative service that will permit friends and family to participate more actively than a formal service allows. Some people may even want to design a ceremony-within-a-ceremony to accommodate those needs.

One choice is to design an entire service. Many of the services we attended were intensely creative, drawing their inspirations and themes from the life's work or important contributions of the person who had died. But another choice is to merge creative elements with a more traditional service.

For example, a memorial service for a forest ranger could be held in a national park for friends who associate her with her work. Or the service could be made simpler and accessible to more people by holding a traditional service closer to home but ending it with a tree-planting ceremony. At an informal service, a small group might choose to join hands to recite a prayer or poem or to share their reminiscences. A larger group might choose a more formalized intimacy, such as a nonreligious "communion service" that includes sharing some symbolic food. People can gather to watch videos created to highlight the major events of their dead friend's life. Another variation, encouraged even by some very formal churches, is the creation of a "memory table" of photographs and other memorabilia. It doesn't play a role in the service but can be viewed by those who attend it.

WHAT ARE THE ADVANTAGES OF A CREATIVE SERVICE?

Because their tone is less formal, creative services can be more spontaneous and personal. For example, many people who have held informal services stressed that rather than limiting the number of speakers, they did the opposite. They encouraged as many people as possible to come forward and make their often extemporaneous remarks. Such services can more easily accommodate participation by those who attend. They can be held in more informal locations, such as a park, a beach, or a forest. And because they can make much more use of the symbols of a deceased person's life, people may find them far more personally evocative.

WHAT ARE THE DISADVANTAGES OF A CREATIVE SERVICE?

Even more than a secular service, a creative, informal service runs the risk of seeming like a random, unfocused gathering. A jam session in memory of a departed musician friend may be intensely moving, or it may seem like just another jam session. It may lack the sense of moment, mourning, and celebration that a memorial service should provide.

An informal service may also seem too unemotional. "It wasn't enough," lamented one woman after a memorial gathering for her dead brother. Since the man, abhorring ceremony, had specifically requested that no service be held, his relatives had simply gathered in a restaurant for an evening of reminiscing. But the event had left the participants feeling hollow and unfinished.

Another danger is that, without a more formal pace and structure, an informal service can become too intense. Listen to the reaction of someone who in a very short time attended many services for friends who had died of AIDS:

> Memorial services! God, how I hate memorial services. I used to go to them all the time, but now unless the person was really special in life I can't bear it. . . . It used to bother me—the services that proceeded in a ritualistic way. I preferred the ones where they sang a special song or read a poem or whatever. But then I went to the service of a friend, a dear friend, and they played a tape he had made explicitly for the event. It was eerie. It was almost cruel. After that I began to appreciate the services that are more, well, impersonal.*

When Judy Augustine and her skydiving club planned a service for a group of friends who had all died together in a plane crash, they deliberately selected lighter music. "The various songs that people chose were really heartfelt, but we stayed away from songs that were extremely emotional," she said. "It was already too much. The pain was so incredible, people could just take so much. We didn't want to send anybody into hysteria."

What's more, an informal service runs the risk of simply not going over very well. People may find the creative ceremonies strange or may not understand how to participate. At one service, a woman spontaneously tried to organize the children in the group to come up front and sing "The Circle of Life" from the movie *The Lion King*. But none of the children knew the words, and they found her impromptu talk on life and death baffling.

Thus, in planning an informal and creative service it is especially important to know the people who will be participating. It may be that more explanation of the service than usual is necessary. Or it may be that some elements you might like to incorporate will be inappropriate for the group as a whole, no matter how moving they may seem to you.

*Madeleine Blais, "I Never Knew Whether I Could Let Go," *The Washington Post*, January 26, 1992, p. W6.

WHERE SHOULD IT BE HELD?

Anywhere. In fact, it is location that often lends informal services their creative, moving tone. Services have been held on farms for those who spent their lives there, in forests, on boats, on golf courses, in fire stations, in shopping malls, and in midair. A Presbyterian minister remembered officiating at one service in the middle of Long Island Sound and at another that was held at the deceased person's favorite fishing hole. A service for a major-league umpire was held in a baseball stadium. A service for a famous clown was held in a circus tent. The procession to the cemetery was in the form of a circus parade with a band and all the circus animals. "Circus animals are considered part of the circus family," said Dominique Jando of the Big Apple Circus. We even found one service that was held, incongruously but poignantly, in a Laundromat.

Think about the places that were special to the person who has died. Some of those places might be beautiful, such as a golf course or a beach. But don't fail to consider other kinds of places. Sometimes the gritty character of a place may be most evocative of the deceased person's character—or of the tragedy of his death. One community held a memorial service for a young girl in the very street where she had been gunned down. A service for a mechanic might be held among the machines he spent his life maintaining; or for an architect at the construction site of a work in progress.

Consider whatever permissions might be necessary. For a small gathering—say, no more than two dozen people—probably no permission is necessary to hold a quiet service in most public places. If you are expecting more people and are planning on gathering in a public place, you should check first to make sure there will be no unexpected interruptions. State and federal parks are used to hosting large gatherings, but many do require advance notice or permits for big groups. You will, of course, need permission for any gathering on private property. Most people we spoke to found it surprisingly easy to obtain permission from sympathetic and amenable owners.

If you have chosen a nontraditional location, make sure there will be easy access and convenient parking and that there won't be any conflicts with neighbors or surrounding business or other traffic. Also make sure that everyone will be able to get to the service. If there is to be a great deal of walking, you may want to arrange help for elderly people or others for whom the trip to the site might pose a problem.

WHEN SHOULD IT BE HELD?

If it is to be the only memorial service held, or if it is also to serve as the funeral, the same time frame applies to informal, creative services as to all other services. The funeral service should be held within a few days after the death and the memorial service ideally no more than two weeks later.

But people also choose to use informal, creative services to mark other important milestones. About twenty-five people held a ceremony to mark the one-year anniversary of the death of a close friend. They chose a remote location on New York's East Side, built a bonfire, and then burned some of the deceased's possessions. They stood around the fire, drinking wine and reminiscing about their friend.

Some religions prescribe that mourning services be held at specific times throughout the year after death. The Jewish community marks periods of mourning—seven days, thirty days, and eleven months after death and then an annual ceremony on the death date. Buddhists also prescribe memorial services at various time periods. Their services are held on the forty-ninth day after death and then on the first, third, seventh, thirteenth, twenty-fifth, thirty-third, and fiftieth anniversary of death. Some Buddhists even perform a hundred-year memorial service.

These extended services can serve a useful psychological purpose in the mourning process. Thus, some people may hold a poetry reading on the anniversary date of the publication of their loved one's first book. They may choose to gather to plant a tree on her birthday. Or they may have an informal remembrance service on Mother's Day, Father's Day, or some other holiday that was particularly meaningful.

CEREMONIES

Many creative and informal memorial services include a ceremony-within-a-ceremony. Here are a few such ceremonies for informal services, which can also be adapted for more formal secular services.

A CANDLELIGHTING

There are several variations of a candlelighting ceremony:

• Place a large candle at the front of the service and give everyone in attendance a small candle. At some time during the service, one person, perhaps a close relative or close friend, lights the large candle while speaking of the memories that he or she has of the deceased. Then all in attendance come forward in turn to light their small candles from the large candle and speak their words of remembrance, if they choose to do so, perhaps beginning with the repeated phrase "I remember her for her . . ." then adding something personal.

• Give each person at the service a candle. Then, at some time during the service, one person lights a candle and offers the flame to another person. All in turn light their candles from the candle of the person next to them, passing the light around the room. This may be accompanied by a repeated sentence of remembrance, such as "We promise to guard the flame of her memory."

• Arrange a bank of candles at the front of the service, making sure there is one candle for each person in attendance. As the service begins, have each person come forward in turn and, using a single lighted taper, light one of the bank of candles. These candles will continue to burn, providing a backdrop for everything else that happens during the service.

A COMMUNION SERVICE

Unlike the sharing of consecrated bread and wine, which in Catholic and Episcopal churches has a sacramental meaning, an informal communion can stress community, sharing, and memories.

• *Bread:* During the service, pass loaves of bread around to all in attendance and let each person break off and eat a small piece. This can be accompanied by a brief, repeated statement such as "We share this bread as we share our memory of _____." Alternatively, you could break the bread into pieces before the service and pass it in baskets.

• *Flowers:* Prepare a basket of flowers—perhaps flowers the deceased liked very much, or else hardy flowers such as daisies. At some point during the services, pass the basket around the room and ask everyone to take a flower in memory of the deceased. Alternatively, have baskets of flowers available to those who enter the service. Ask people to take a flower and hold it until some point in the service when they can come forward and place their flowers into a memorial that has been prepared. Some possibilities: a wide-weave burlap hanging or a form that has been covered with medium-mesh chicken wire (the wire will be covered with the flowers).

• *Balloons:* At an outdoor service, give everyone a helium-filled balloon to hold, and, at a designated point in the service, ask them to release the balloons. At a large gathering, in particular, the balloons soaring away have a very dramatic and moving effect. Alternatively, you might have a large bunch of balloons which can all be released by one person at some point in the service.

A PLANTING

Planting trees, shrubs, or flowers, even scattering grass seed, is a good way of remembering someone who loved the out-of-doors. Planting a tree, especially, is a fine commemoration, since it will provide a lasting, permanent memorial. Such a memorial is also particularly appropriate for those who are cremated and choose to have their ashes scattered. They leave no place loved ones can visit, and a tree can take the place of a grave for this purpose.

• *Tree planting:* A tree planting can be part of a longer service, or it can be the focal point of the service. It will suggest the natural cycle of life and death and the renewal of life in the face of death. For this service, it is important to choose a pleasant location, one where the tree will be welcomed and which loved ones can easily visit. Make arrangements to have the tree delivered to the site. Consider also whether to include the digging of the hole for the tree in the service or to have the hole prepared to receive the tree. Those closest to the deceased can plant the tree at the appropriate time during the service, and everyone present can take turns dropping a shovelful of dirt around the roots.

• *Shrub planting:* A service to plant a shrub is similar to a tree-planting service. But as an alternative, the actual planting can be secondary to the creation of a memorial. Pass out bright-colored squares of paper and pencils to everyone at the service and ask them to write down their memories of the deceased. Then, at some point in the service, they can come forward one by one and hang their paper squares on the shrub (you can use Christmas-ornament hooks or string).

• *Flower planting:* Have enough peat pots filled with living flowers available for each person in attendance. At the end of the service, invite everyone to take a pot, return home, and plant the flower in a meaningful place.

• *Grass or wildflower planting:* During the service, pass trays of grass seed or the seeds of wildflowers. Then, at the conclusion of the service, invite everyone to scatter the seeds to the wind. This can be quite dramatic, especially if the service is held in a wide-open space or someplace else where the seeds will actually sow.

A COMMUNITY SERVICE

Sometimes a community, especially a very close-knit one, will want to hold a ceremony to remember everyone who has died in the past year. Any of the above ceremonies can be adapted to memorialize more than one person. Each member of the community may be invited to the front to light a candle in memory of a specific person, for example. Or each may hang the name of an individual person on the tree or shrub before planting. In another variation of a community service, people are invited to speak the name of each dead person out loud.

DOING SOMETHING TOGETHER

For a small group of people who have been involved in some activity together, nothing is more natural than to incorporate that activity into the memorial service. It may be as dramatic as the airborne memorial service the Peninsula Skydivers Club held for the twelve people who were killed in a small-plane crash. Or it may be as quiet as a knitting club getting together to create a pattern in memory of one of its members.

• *A poetry reading:* Many people, and not just professional poets, gather together to read their own works. A memorial service might follow the same format as a group reading. Wine, coffee, or a meal might be served and each member of the group might read a poem she has written, either earlier or perhaps even as a special tribute to the dead person.

• A *jam session:* With both memorial poetry readings and jam sessions, the role of the performance is different from what it is in a more formal service. In a formal service, the music or reading is an accompaniment to the service. In an informal service, the people who found those activities most important perform or read them as a unique way of remembering the deceased. Churches can get involved, too. One church in Manhattan, Saint Peter's Church on Lexington Avenue, has held more than three hundred jazz services. "They're very improvisational," said Pastor Dale Lind. From Dizzy Gillespie to Miles Davis to Stan Getz, jazz players get together to memorialize their idols and friends. But such a service isn't just for famous musicians. Even people whose musical talent is limited to an informal community group like to remember one of their own this way.

When music is played at a service for a musician who has died, it is usually music that he composed or performed. So the program grows out of the person being memorialized. And the people who perform at memorial services are those who performed with the deceased or who knew him well. Sometimes people will spontaneously rise and speak. Sometimes the music will flow spontaneously.

• A *memorial walk:* You can make use of a place that was special to the person who died. If she was a golfer, gather and walk the course together and share stories about her life. If she was a hiker, walk some scenic route. If she was someone important to the town, walk through the town and talk about the things she did to make it a better place.

THINGS TO SEE AND THINGS TO TOUCH

A MEMORY TABLE

A memory table can play as central or as peripheral a role as you like. Set up a table either at the back of the service or, if you plan to incorporate it into the ceremony, in a more centrally located spot. On that table you can place things that were important to the deceased person's life. These things can be as special or as ordinary as you wish. For a carpenter or a mechanic, you might display the tools of the trade. Was he a collector? Display items from his collection. Or some special items associated with a sport he enjoyed: a hunter's cap or fishing gear; the golf ball he saved from a hole in one; the baseball Roger Maris autographed for him many years ago. What was important to the person's life? What kinds of things would other people most associate with him? A memory table can also be a testimony to the person's talent or hobbies. Was she a craftswoman? Display her work. Did she weave? Put her weavings around the room. Was she an artist? Hang her watercolors.

A LIFE COLLAGE

Though similar to a memory table, a life collage aims to tell a story. In chronological order around the room, display things that were important to the deceased person's life, things she had been keeping because of the memories they evoked: pictures of her parents, her birth certificate, the doll she saved from her childhood, her report card, pictures from her prom, the newspaper clipping announcing her engagement, the newspaper story in which she is quoted as an expert on some subject, programs from the plays and operas she loved attending, the announcement of her wedding, her professional awards, pictures of her family. Such a display will tell the story of her life in all its facets.

A VIDEO

The ease with which you can now transfer photos to video makes a video life collage possible. Assemble a collection of pictures, which you can either film yourself or turn over to a professional. There are many firms now that for a very modest fee will film a twenty-minute collection of pictures and dub in the background music of your choice.

You can use pictures from just one facet of the deceased person's life. For example, if she was a member of a bowling team, you could assemble photos of your group bowling or celebrating together. Or, if you are a family member, you could create a video of her entire life. Many people find either one of these choices extremely moving, especially when coupled with music that has some meaning for friends and family.

Don't shy away from even informal shots. One minister recalled a family's memory table that included a picture of the deceased wearing swimming trunks and holding a can of beer. It was exactly the way people remembered him. "It was a comfort for the family," the minister said. "The photo showed him doing what was natural for him."

Another video possibility is to tape the service itself. While many people are already quite comfortable with audiotaping such a service, many still shy away from the more intrusive videotaping. Those who have done so, though, say they found it useful since they were often too emotionally overwhelmed to remember the details of the service.

A PHOTO EXCHANGE

A service can be built around photos that people have of the person who has died. Invite them to gather and bring with them several pictures showing some activity they shared. Each member of the group can talk about those memories and their meaning.

Another possibility is to give out photos. One family of a person who had died went through his photo album and pulled out pictures of him with each of his close friends. The family then had those pictures copied and handed out to those friends at the memorial service.

A MEMORIAL TRIBUTE

"Fill up the saucer 'til it overflows . . ." That's a line from the haunting funeral song in George Gershwin's opera *Porgy and Bess*. In many cultures, the "saucer" is an integral part of a funeral service. Without the contributions dropped into it, the family would have no means of providing a proper burial.

Contributions are once again becoming an important part of funerals and memorial services. That's especially true as people increasingly turn away from expensive floral displays and seek some more fitting way of honoring the deceased. Sometimes it is a contribution to a charity that was important to the person who has died. If the person was actively involved in youth sports, the family may designate a league that is collecting scholarship money. Or, if the person died of cancer, a contribution to the American Cancer Society might be appropriate.

Some people may want to do more than that, however. Teachers may want to band together to raise funds to create a scholarship fund in the name of their deceased colleague. Doctors and nurses may want to create a fund to buy a major piece of equipment for their hospital. Writers may collaborate on a book about the disease from which their friend died. Politically active people may want to designate some project to undertake in the name of their friend or relative.

PLANNING YOUR OWN SERVICE

Just as some people may not want a memorial service, others want to have a hand in planning their own. Few people, of course, plan the service while they are in the full flush of life. But for the elderly or those with a terminal illness, planning their own service gives them a sense of control and an opportunity to review their lives and involve the people they love most in remembering them.

You can pick your own minister and church or some other celebrant and a location that is important to you. You can select favorite readings, pick music from your own collection of tapes and CDs, or ask your musical friends to perform at the service. If you have been ill and dependent on caregivers, planning your own service will give you the opportunity to express your feelings toward them. It will also be a great help to those you leave behind. It will simplify their job and give them the satisfaction of knowing that they are carrying out your wishes.

If you do plan your own service, however, keep in mind that you will not be there to participate. You should be aware that the people who will be participating have just suffered a loss—the loss of you. And they may find very intense emotional moments too much to bear. In particular, those we interviewed talked about taped messages, which many found too emotionally grueling. One man, a singer, sang and taped the songs for his memorial service himself. His survivors found listening to the tape almost unbearably painful.

ASHES

Many nontraditional services revolve around scattering ashes because people frequently ask to have their ashes scattered in nontraditional places. Lakes, golf courses, mountains, vacation homes, even busy city streets are all places where people have, for reasons personal to them, asked for their ashes to be scattered.

Some places have ordinances that prohibit the scattering of ashes. You may wish to inquire. But in many cases, discretion is all that is required. The cremated remains are hygienic and pose no health or environmental hazard. A discreet scattering bypasses the bureaucratic morass that could emerge from a request for permission, especially if there actually is no ordinance specifically prohibiting scattering ashes.

People who have scattered their relatives' ashes have two observations, however. One is that the ashes aren't, strictly speaking, ashes; they are uncombusted bone fragments, and you should be aware that they may remain wherever they have been scattered in recognizable form for years.

Ashes are often buried in a grave—a family plot or a site chosen by the deceased or his family and friends—and the site is customarily marked like a traditional grave. If ashes are scattered in some remote place—over a lake, for example—many people later regret that there is no grave or place to visit. That is why the scattering of ashes is often combined with a tree planting.

A CHECKLIST FOR PLANNING
AN INFORMAL, CREATIVE SERVICE

____ Where will you hold the service?

____ What about logistical considerations?

- Is there parking?

- Is access good?

- Do you need permission?

- What if it rains?

____ When will you hold the service?

- Close to the funeral?

- Instead of a funeral?

- To mark an anniversary?

—— Are you planning anything really unusual?

  • Will the rest of the community find it moving?

  • Should you explain the service to those who won't find it familiar?

—— Are there other ceremonies you might want to incorporate?

  • Candlelighting?

  • Communion?

  • Tree planting?

—— Are there activities you can share?

  • Playing music?

  • Reading poetry?

  • Taking a memorial walk?

  • Contributions to charity?

  • Taking on a community project?

—— Are there memorabilia you would like to share?

  • Crafts?

  • Writing?

  • Poetry?

  • Photographs?

  • Are there memorabilia you would like to ask guests to bring to share?

—— Would you like to tape the service?

  • Audiotape?

  • Videotape?

—— Will you bury the ashes or scatter them?

  • Will a ceremony accompany the burial or scattering?

CHAPTER SEVEN

MEMORABLE INFORMAL, CREATIVE SERVICES

A SERVICE IN A LAUNDROMAT

For more than thirty years Margaret Wosser ran a coin-operated Laundromat in the Castro section of San Francisco. She befriended the people there, a diverse collection of students, immigrants, shopkeepers, retirees, and panhandlers. The Laundromat became a place to congregate. She raffled off turkeys, televisions, and VCRs to help the people in the neighborhood. And when she died, she left $1.8 million, nearly all of which was to be used on outreach programs in the neighborhood.

The Reverend Robert McCann, a pastor at the church that would administer the gift, set out to create a memorial to Mrs. Wosser. "It seemed appropriate to have it in the Laundromat where she spent an awful lot of her time," he recalled. Although she had left her money to a church, she was not a church person. A service in the Laundromat, moreover, would give the people who had been most touched by her life a better chance to attend and participate.

Which they did. The Laundromat was on the ground floor of a Victorian-type house on a very busy corner of the neighborhood. Word spread quickly, and nearly seventy people arrived at the appropriate time. Spontaneously, everything necessary for a service appeared. A friend drew a pastel likeness of Mrs. Wosser and put it into the Laundromat window. Some people brought flowers. Others brought candlesticks. And still others brought table linen which they spread over the laundry folding table to create a makeshift altar.

The service itself was a standard Episcopal service. There were prayers from the Book of Common Prayer and a modified Episcopal liturgy. Mr. McCann gave a eulogy during which he explained to the group how the money Mrs. Wosser had left behind would be used, and because Mrs. Wosser had frequently thrown pizza parties for the neighborhood, the service concluded with pizza for everyone.

"Prayer and pizza—people loved it," said Mr. McCann. "We got so many wonderful calls and comments afterwards about how nice it was that the church came to where she was."

A MIDAIR MEMORIAL SERVICE

One day in September 1995, a Beechcraft Queen Air crashed shortly after taking off from an airport in Virginia, killing ten sport parachutists, a pilot, and one man on the ground. Two weeks later, members of the Peninsula Flying Club conducted a midair display to memorialize their departed friends.

Nearly seven hundred people gathered on the field and watched as plane after plane took off. The first five carried the ashes of five of the skydivers who had chosen to be cremated. "It's a common practice," among skydivers, said Judy Augustine, vice president of the club, explaining that skydivers like to have their ashes scattered from the skies with their friends watching. "Skydivers have so many friends that everybody wants to come and give their last respects and say good-bye."

The closest friend of each deceased skydiver carried his or her ashes and scattered them. For the people who were buried, multicolored rose petals were dropped from another plane. For one pair of skydivers who had been partners, twenty skydivers did a swan dive in formation and scattered their ashes in free fall. The children of one diver went up in a plane and dropped their father's ashes from its door. At a final moment, twelve skydivers with twelve flags attached to their ankles jumped, joined hands, then let go of one another and dropped separately to the ground. The divers then folded the flags to give to the families of those who had died. The people who had been chosen to dive felt they had done something meaningful for their friends. "It helped a lot," said Ms. Augustine.

On the ground, a podium and tables and chairs were set up. One table displayed a photo of each skydiver who had died and flower arrangements. There was a program to explain the service and to let people know whose ashes were being dropped when, and from which plane.

It was decided not to limit the eulogies but rather to allow everyone who had known one of the skydivers to speak. In all, about twelve or thirteen people spoke. "How do you get over people who shared the same dreams?" asked Ms. Augustine. "These were people who were lovers of life."

Only one aspect of the service was "a little bit religious," said Ms. Augustine. One of the men who had been killed had been a minister. His sister, who was also a minister, delivered a sermon. But apart from that, the rest of the service, and the eulogies, were secular. "They talked about the love they had for [the people who died] and that hopefully they are in a better place. It was one of the most beautiful things I have ever experienced," said Ms. Augustine. Like many other memorial services, it had been planned quickly. "We had less than a week to put it together."

A RIVERBOAT SERVICE FOR A LOCAL FIGURE

Benjamin Bernstein was a well-known figure around Cincinnati. He owned the Mike Fink Riverboat Restaurant, which sat on the Ohio River just outside the city. He was so active in the community that he had been named "Ambassador of Cincinnati" just before he died.

Mr. Bernstein was cremated, and his ashes were buried. Rather than a funeral, the family held a small private service at the graveside. The later memorial service, however, reflected his status as a public figure around Cincinnati. It was held on the riverboat. The family was not at all religious. In fact, "We were areligious," said Shirley Bernstein, his wife. So religious symbols were few. There was a rabbi present—"We allowed him to read the Twenty-third Psalm," said Mrs. Bernstein.

The rest of the service was secular. A military unit in ceremonial dress stood on the banks of the river and fired a salute. One of Mr. Bernstein's sons read a letter he had written to his father two or three months before he had died, thanking him for everything he had done. But the two major factors in the service were the river itself and the people of the city of Cincinnati. More than three thousand people stood on the boat and the docks and crowded onto the banks above to be present. "There was a huge crowd. It was a great tribute to his life," said Mrs. Bernstein. "Some people stood out in the cold on the steps on Riverside Drive for a hour to get in."

Mr. Bernstein had requested that his ashes be poured into the river. The family did so, pouring most of the ashes into a ring of gardenias floating on the water. (Mrs. Bernstein had kept some of the ashes from the earlier burial.) "The river was a symbol of his life," she said.

A SERVICE WITH VIDEO

For her husband, Leo Weisse, his wife, Rosemarie, arranged a simple gathering. The focus was a video of scenes from his life. "I didn't know what to do about a service for Leo," she said. "We were not religious. The only thing to do was pictures and a video of him." She and her children collected pictures spanning several decades. A professional service transferred them to video and added Vivaldi's "The Four Seasons" as accompanying music. She carried the ashes to the grave site at Fort Logan National Cemetery in Denver, where about a hundred people were gathered. Leo and Rosemarie's son Mitchell read the only eulogy. There were no hymns, no Bible readings, no prayers. Without a religious element, the service was very short, under half an hour.

After the service, the group went to a restaurant owned by some friends and showed the video in a private room. Leo had been involved in the trucking industry most of his life. He had been an earthy person, fond of off-color jokes, beer, and camaraderie. Some of the photos used in the video reflected this side of him. People attending this part of the service responded well, cracking jokes and carrying on a light repartee while the video was running. They thought the service was very appropriate to Leo. "It was nice," she said. "It was not obsessively sad, like those where a body is present."

CHAPTER EIGHT

THE EULOGY

One of the best-known, most-often-quoted passages from Shakespeare begins a literary eulogy in *Julius Caesar*, when Mark Antony speaks of his murdered friend:

> *Friends, Romans, countrymen, lend me your ears.*
> *I come to bury Caesar, not to praise him.*

It is a stirring, dramatic speech as, despite his opening promise, Antony proceeds to praise Caesar effusively, to condemn his enemies, and to rouse the people of Rome against them.

Eulogies need not be as full of historical moment nor as laden with political meaning as this one. But they can easily be as stirring and as meaningful. Indeed, eulogies—literally, "good words"—are often the cornerstone of a memorial service. They can provide solace to the bereaved, courage and inspiration to other listeners, and pride and satisfaction to the speaker. And they can do it not as Mark Antony did, through the ringing use of rhetoric, but rather through simple, heartfelt recollection. Let's look at eulogies from two perspectives: that of the family planning the service and that of the person actually delivering the eulogy.

IF YOU ARE PLANNING THE SERVICE

WHOM SHOULD YOU ASK TO SPEAK?

The decision may be based on many factors, some of them obvious, some not. You should first consider all the people you think were meaningful in the life of your loved one. An opportunity to speak at a memorial service is a great honor and a recognition of the importance someone has played in the life of another. You should ask them to speak, even if you think they may decline.

For one thing, they may want to contribute in some other way. Only the rabbi spoke at the service for Sheldon Dickstein, although his wife, Ruth, asked many people to speak. "They wrote me later saying they were too overcome to speak in front of others," she said. Instead, they shared their reminiscences with the rabbi, who included them in his eulogy.

For another thing, people who are asked to speak will be proud of that fact whether or not they accept. Moreover, even the shyest person may surprise you and choose to speak if asked. Who are logical choices? Family members, of course, as well as professional colleagues, best friends, and members of organizations to which the deceased belonged. If he was someone of importance in the community, ask community leaders to speak. Or if she was important in her field, another leader in that field might be appropriate.

You may also want to consider people for their public speaking skills and presence. A funeral or memorial service is not theater, of course. But a highly emotionally charged service before a large group of people will certainly benefit from a speaker who is poised, commanding, and prepared to take the podium with confidence.

HOW SHOULD THE EULOGIES BE ARRANGED?

You should briefly interview each speaker to make sure that the eulogies will not be repetitive. The lead speaker is often the person who has known the deceased the longest and can provide the broadest context for his life. Many people like to reserve the final eulogy for a family member, who can not only provide a more personal note at the end but can also thank the speakers and those attending.

HOW MUCH TIME SHOULD YOU ALLOW FOR EULOGIES?

There are two schools of thought. One is that the total time for eulogies should be limited to about twenty minutes to keep the time for the entire service under an hour. For formal and religious services in particular, there is a practical reason for this. An hour seems to be just about the right amount of time to hold people's attention and to provide a suitably dignified service.

The second school of thought is that a memorial service is just that— a service to the community. Thus, anyone who wishes to speak should be allowed to do so. Indeed, there are many services at which not only are speakers arranged in advance but a general invitation is issued at the end of the service for anyone to come forward who wishes to speak.

IF YOU ARE DELIVERING THE EULOGY

Many people worry about delivering a eulogy. It may be one of the few times they will rise to address a large group. Moreover, added to the usual worries about speaking in public is the emotional weight of grief. People worry that they will break down, be unable to finish, or forget what they are about to say.

The most important thing to remember about a eulogy is that it is a gift. A gift for you to be able to speak about a family member or friend before those who also loved and respected him. A gift of memory for everyone to share. It is not a performance, nor will it be judged as such. Your job is to be thoughtful and genuine, not to be Johnny Carson.

Nonetheless, some simple rules about public speaking serve as well in this setting as in any other. Here are a few.

There is an old acronym that is applied to public speaking: "KISS," meaning Keep It Short and Simple. Eulogies should be kept to about five minutes in length. That's enough time for an opening remark, about three brief anecdotes or stories, and a closing remark. Most people worry that they will run out of things to say. The reality is the opposite. Five minutes go by amazingly quickly. If you are writing your eulogy, plan on about four pages of typed, double-spaced text. That's about a thousand words.

As for the content of the eulogy, don't feel that you need to strive for profundity or beautiful metaphor. The most telling eulogies are the simplest ones. At her father's service, one young woman spoke about a Valentine she had received every year from a secret admirer. They had come to her around the world, including in Frankfurt during the year she was stationed there with the Army. Of course, the Valentines had come from her father. At Stephen Tudor's memorial service, one person spoke about his ability to fix things, including a screwball computer. Another talked about a sailing trip when Steve had slept through a storm while he and a third man had struggled with the boat. They had had to wake him up, and he had handled the situation expertly.

Think about things that were characteristic of the deceased. One person ended his eulogy with a jaunty "Toodle-loo!" That was the way his friend had always ended their conversations. Do you remember an evening from your childhood, catching fireflies together? Tell about it. Did he help you once when you needed it badly? Now is the time to thank him. The more specific the anecdote, the more likely it is to be meaningful.

Ideally, you want to tell stories that show the best and most characteristic sides of the person who has died: his attributes as a husband and father, how he practiced kindness, how he helped others, his contributions to his community. Don't shy away from anecdotes that show, perhaps, his eccentric side or some little foible. But make sure such stories are tempered with affection. Also, make sure that the focus of the anecdote is on the deceased, not on you. Don't tell lengthy anecdotes in which clever things you said to him are prominently featured. And avoid stories that show how important you were in his life. *He* is the reason family and friends have gathered here. *You* should be a supporting player.

Don't avoid using his name for fear of hurting the family. They know he is gone. Nor do you need to use circumlocutions for death. Everyone knows he has died. It is much easier and more natural just to come out and say, for example, "the night before John died" than to struggle with an unnatural euphemism.

When you deliver the eulogy, do so with dignity. Speak slowly and deliberately. Do not rush through your talk. Use short, simple sentences, and enunciate each word clearly. Stand directly facing the audience. Do not clutch the podium or move your hands and feet unnecessarily. Look directly at the audience and speak to them. If you are reading your speech, look up at the audience after every phrase or sentence. Remember, you are giving them a gift—the gift of your knowledge and perception of a person they loved.

What if you do break down? People will forgive you. They will understand that you, like they, are overcome with the feeling of loss. The family will perhaps even be comforted to know that you so strongly share their grief. Take a moment to compose yourself and go on. If you cannot, simply step down and let the next person carry on.

USING HUMOR

"I think humor in a memorial service is good psychology and good theology. People in grief find joy and healing in humor," said Robert Lee, pastor of the First Congregational Church in Burlington, Vermont. When people hear amusing anecdotes, he adds, they say: " 'My God, I never expected to laugh.' But that's how the deceased was."

Over and over again, the people we interviewed spoke of the healing role of humor. Frequently, the reason was that humor had played an important role in the deceased's life. "Once I was asked to do the eulogy for a man who was a genuinely funny person," said Craig Bustrin, a priest at Saint Michael's Episcopal Church in New York. "It was impossible not to share that with the people at the service."

In many services, humor coexists with grief. "In one memorial service, the deceased was portrayed as a man joking, full of life. He had so enjoyed telling stories and jokes," said John Mackie at the Unitarian Universalist Church of Atlanta. "All the stories people told were humorous. People cried out of grief there. But they felt if you knew him, you knew that he wouldn't have wanted people moaning over him. We talked about missing him and how he'd made them laugh."

But what kind of humor is appropriate for a memorial service? It should be humor that is affectionate and illuminates something about the person who has died. You can talk about humorous foibles, but those foibles should be ones that his family and friends are aware of. Did he have trouble reading maps? You could tell a story about a disastrous road trip you took together. Did he have a terrible singing voice? Tell about the time your college buddies banded together and took up a collection to get him to stop singing. Did he enjoy practical jokes? Talk about the time he put an advertisement for a very cheap Harley-Davidson in the newspaper—and included your phone number.

To be avoided, of course, are jokes and humorous anecdotes that reflect badly on his character or comportment, stories that would embarrass anyone else present, and racist or sexist humor. You should also avoid ribald stories and vulgar language unless you are speaking to a small group of intimates and you are all used to that sort of thing. Indeed, we found, surprisingly, that many people appreciated a judicious bit of vulgarity in a service for someone who was well known for his crude language and off-color jokes. This type of thing must be handled with very special care, however, since the line dividing the mildly scandalous—and therefore appreciated—from the offensive is very fine.

THE PROBLEM PERSON

There is an old saying: "We never bury anyone but a saint."

But what if the person who died was not a saint? No one is, of course. But what if he truly was a problem to those around him? It was once the custom to ignore his actual life and deeds and to eulogize someone who never existed, which resulted in much seat-squirming and a general feeling of unease. Nowadays, people find that directness is more appreciated and better tolerated. But it must be directness with a purpose and with compassion.

How to eulogize a person who has caused pain to those around him depends somewhat on the nature of the problem. Sometimes omitting mention of the pain is the happiest solution. One woman had for many years suffered from Alzheimer's disease, which had destroyed any semblance of the person her family had once known. Caring for her had exhausted her family and friends. Her death had been a blessing for everyone concerned.

Yet by skipping over that pain—acknowledging it briefly and then moving on—those who gave eulogies were able to magically restore the person her family and friends had once known. They spoke of her as a young woman, as a mother, as a colleague, as a friend. They told stories that showed her not as an invalid but as a vigorous, caring woman. Without ever really mentioning her sufffering and the years of hard work in caring for her, the stories of her earlier life helped put that difficult time into perspective.

In other cases, eulogies can acknowledge that joy and pain often coexist. Consider the directness of a ten-year-old, Chloë Malle, the daughter of film director Louis Malle: "I loved him, but sometimes I wanted to kill him," she said at his memorial service.*

One person, struggling to speak at the service for a man who had killed himself, found that he could still talk about happier times: "His taking his life doesn't negate the joy and zest and vitality with which he lived and which he gave to others. We need to be reminded of that. It is essential that we remember."

We found that many very moving eulogies dealt directly with the ambivalence of the person's relationships with the deceased. People spoke of competition, of irascibility, of difficult periods they had gone through together, of the pain his absence or divorce had caused. These recollections could easily have been too raw, too emotional, too personal for a large gathering. They could easily have broken down into bathos and feelings of pity. They all worked, however, because they were recollections tempered with affection and understanding. They were leavened by a sense that everyone's life is filled with vicissitudes and that every person's character includes some darkness as well as light.

Indeed, many pastors spoke of the surprising depth of emotion that was evoked at services even for people who appeared to others to be brutal or remote. "I learned that there is no telling," said one pastor. "I have seen half-hour services grow into two-hour services for people I would have supposed were disliked. I learned that no one can tell who is important to another."

The funeral and memorial service can also be a time for strange and lovely reconciliations. The Irish short-story writer Seán O'Faoláin wrote of one such: A dead man's mistress alarms the people of a small village by making plain her intent to attend the service. People wait in horror as they anticipate the inevitable conflict between the longtime mistress and the long-suffering wife. Instead, the two women collapse into each other's arms, joined at least for a moment in sorrow for the man they both have lost.

But what about a person—such as an alcoholic father who ended up

*Robert McG. Thomas, Jr., "Tribute to Louis Malle," *The New York Times*, March 1, 1996, p. B-7.

living on the street—whose flaws go beyond mere peccadillos? What about the abusive parent, whose children still feel the scars well into adulthood? What about the person whose contentiousness sowed anger everywhere he went? A eulogy for such a difficult person may stretch the bounds of charity. But, as many people have found, it can also be redemptive. It would be almost impossible for those speaking not to talk honestly and directly about the pain the person has caused. But their eulogies can also be uplifting and helpful, if there is an attempt at understanding and forgiveness and a realization that underneath even the most profound anger at another person, there is love—or else there would be no anger. (There are several examples of this in Chapter 9.)

THE PROBLEM SPEAKER

Are there people you should not let speak? Sometimes. The death of a loved one often uncovers long-buried angers, hurts, and resentments. Just as there are problem people among the dead, so too are there people whose problems with the person who died still fester.

Many funeral and memorial services have been blighted by people who used them to air their personal grievances. A eulogy is not the occasion for hashing out sibling rivalries, proselytizing one's own religious beliefs to a reluctant audience, or settling old scores. There is a fine line between the direct expression of the pain the deceased has caused and the personal expression of a private hurt. The test must be whether the complaint is of general relevance to everyone gathered at the service. A eulogy is, after all, a public expression. Painful sentiments can be expressed, but only if they will have meaning to the group as a whole.

You should do everything you can to keep such personal pain private. Encourage the would-be speaker to channel his anger in another way— in private conversations, for example, or counseling. But what if someone with a legitimate right to speak—a sibling or a child—persists? What if a speaker says things about the deceased that family and friends find unpleasant, offensive, or untrue? Such a eulogy could easily be divisive and become the focal point of the service. Your only recourse is to try to apply the same virtues to the living as to the dead: good manners, compassion—and forgiveness.

A CHECKLIST FOR PLANNING
AND DELIVERING EULOGIES

If you are planning the service:

____ Consider who wants to speak.

____ Consider the length of the service.

____ Talk to each potential speaker to eliminate repetition.

____ Make sure each speaker knows the order of the service.

____ If there is to be more than one eulogy, consider selecting people from different periods of the deceased's life.

____ If you want people to speak, ask them, even if you think they may decline.

____ If only the minister or rabbi is to speak, collect reminiscences to enable him to personalize his eulogy.

If you are delivering the eulogy:

____ Keep it short, under six minutes or about one thousand words.

____ Keep it simple. Don't strive for profundity or eloquence.

____ Introduce yourself and give a brief summary of your relationship to the deceased.

____ Choose anecdotes that illuminate the deceased's character and contributions.

____ Use affectionate humor where appropriate.

____ Avoid stories that will, even inadvertently, embarrass family or friends or put the deceased in a bad light.

____ Avoid anecdotes which illustrate the important role you played in the deceased's life. Choose anecdotes which illustrate the important role the deceased played in your life and in the lives of others.

____ Speak slowly and clearly.

— Look at your audience.

— If you lose your composure, give yourself a moment or two to regain it. The audience will understand and will wait for you.

— If you cannot regain your composure, leave the podium.

— Strive to avoid expressions of anger or resentment, even though they may be justified.

CHAPTER NINE

MEMORABLE EULOGIES

A SISTER REMEMBERS
A MAN WHO TOOK HIS OWN LIFE

One of the hardest eulogies to deliver is for someone who has taken his own life. In this eulogy, a sister explains her brother's courage in fighting depression for so many years. And using very simple anecdotes, she shows both sides of the painful intensity with which he lived his life—how it drove him to exhilarating highs of accomplishment and ultimately to an unbearable low.

This was a man who wanted so much to be happy. And to be of service to his family and his community. In a time of much talk about values and ethics, he lived his. He wanted so much from life and demanded so much from himself. In the broadcasting business, we sometimes work with a device called a "compressor limiter." It takes the extreme highs and lows out of the signal. Jeff didn't have one of those. Ever.

When he was about ten years old, we got a *World Book Encyclopedia.* Jeff made it his business to master the signature of every one of the presidents, Washington to Ike. He would trace and then recopy each signature till he got it to perfection. You'd say "Martin Van Buren," and he'd proudly dash off the precise signature. A little later, he befriended the man who operated the old switch tower at the Wilmette station of the

Chicago and Northwestern Railroad. While other kids played kick the can in the alley, Jeff was soaking up railroad lore from an old hand. Even as a kid, he was a seeker of knowledge—and he was consumed by his interests.

When he played golf, he played thirty-six holes a day, frighteningly angry at himself when he didn't meet his own steep standards. When he could play consistently near par, he turned to sailboat racing. It was a boat designed for a crew of two or three, but he rigged his boat so he could head out to the horizon alone, testing himself. He developed complex strategies for each race—and yes, he won the championship, year after year. But despite his intensity he was so gracious that his competitors were his friends. It was kind of an honor to finish second, looking at Jeff's stern.

And then of course came flying. It was the perfect combination for Jeff—a high degree of technical "vector and frequency" stuff combined with spirituality.

All through these passions, music helped Jeff channel his excess intensity. Banging through some Rachmaninoff as an adolescent, playing Buck Owens riffs on his National guitar through his, I think, painful high school years, relaxing into his Dobro and pedal steel guitar in Oregon and Alaska.

Alaska was also a good fit for Jeff. I remember Juneau as something of a haven for energetic, intense eccentrics—long before *Northern Exposure* hit prime time. You could let off a lot of steam up there without anyone noticing. It was a state office building joke that the kicked-around wastebaskets and banged-up phones belonged to Jeff.

I remember flying with Jeff above the glacial fields near Juneau. He pointed the plane straight at a sheer cliff of ice and said, "Okay, now you fly her." I didn't panic. I was with Jeff. Just as it was okay to be out on Lake Michigan with him in a little boat during a big storm. I knew he would handle it. He was my big brother, and a good one.

But when the storms were inside, when the cliffs towered in his own perception, they were overwhelming. He could and did handle and help with all kinds of routine problems and traumatic crises for my parents and me. He has, in fact, handled his own illness for decades (I believe), rising above his self-directed rage to return to the world of the living. He took great joy in his friends, his dog, his career, his music, his flying, my kids, his wife, and his child.

But he was terribly afraid that his depressive illness would affect [his son] Wyatt. With characteristic fervor he tried, with increasing desperation, to set himself right. He read books, listened to tapes, visited churches, talked to ministers, to shrinks, and took medications which may have helped or exacerbated his problems.

But let us try to celebrate his life — to hold on to good memories so that we can pass them on to Wyatt when he wants to know more. We will tell him of a brilliant, intense man who loved his wife and child. A loving, dutiful son, a dependable, delightful friend and brother. My dad remembered this quote from *Hamlet* last Sunday: "Now cracks a noble heart. Good night, sweet prince. And flights of angels sing thee to thy rest."

A EULOGY WITH HUMOR FOR A FUNNY MAN

Here is an example of a perfect, sensitive use of humor. As person after person rose to attest, Tom Tolleson was a very funny man — and a very clever and imaginative one, too. This eulogy is filled with humor — and with a very real affection for and understanding of the man being eulogized.

Good morning. Tom Tolleson — the flying ace. Caroline asked me to address this subject since Tom and I have had so many miraculous experiences. I think he could have been a very successful writer. His imagination was limitless. It was instantaneous. And for the word I've selected, it was outrageous. Like these flowers, they are birds of paradise, his favorite flowers. Caroline put these out front. Aren't they outrageous?

In the locker room and at cocktail parties, Tom was at his best. Many years ago, before I knew what was really going on, Tom began to convince people that he and I were World War Two flying aces. And that we flew our B-17s all over Europe, in and out of enemy flak and at twenty-five thousand feet dodging those German fighters, and he said we flew over fifty missions. Incredible. And he was so convincing I began to believe him, you know? And according to Tom, we had many, many close calls, like in 1944. Somehow, both of our B-17s were shot down over the Rhine River, but we were fortunate to parachute into a wine vineyard, where we crawled into a small cellar, and there were kegs of German Rhine wine and French Beaujolais. We remained hidden in the cellar while we plotted our escape. And Tom said it best: "We ran out of the cellar at the same time the wine ran out."

One of his most creative moments came at a cocktail party some years ago. We were standing and talking to a few friends and strangers. One of them mentioned that he was a retired Navy captain, and he began to talk high-tech Navy stories, and Tom couldn't stand it. And he interrupted soon and took over, and he said, much to my surprise, "David and I were on the *Arizona* when it was sunk at Pearl Harbor, and we were blown into the water and managed to swim ashore—two of the few survivors." Well, he got everybody's attention, especially the Navy captain, who started these technical questions, and Tom said, "You-all excuse me, I'm going to get another drink. David, you take over."

But this is a highlight of Tom's recent life. He came into the locker room so excited—I'd never seen him like this before. He had just come back from New Orleans on a one-hour flight on Delta. And he was in the middle of a couple of younger fellows. And one of them said, "You weren't in World War Two by any chance, were you?" And he said, "Well, as a matter of fact I was, but I'd rather not talk about it." And they said, "Well, please tell us some stories." And he looked at me, and he said, "David, what could I do? They were pleading for war stories." So he said, "For one hour I had some of the fondest memories that I've ever had. I ordered drinks around, and remembered some of my finest experiences." And he laughed, and I laughed.

And when we remember Tom, we will all remember some of our finest experiences. Thank you.

A SIMPLE SPEECH BY A SON

This eulogy shows that even a very simple, direct, unadorned statement can be moving. Here, a son says that although his father's life was a troubled one, he was a good man and much loved by his family.

Thank you all for coming.

I believe everyone here is familiar enough with Leo Weisse to know he didn't like ritual or ceremony. It's out of respect for his values that this memorial service will be brief. On the other hand, I think he was proud of his Air Force experience, and this is why his ashes are being buried here at Fort Logan.

Maybe the best way to memorialize my dad would be to stand here and tell you a bunch of his favorite jokes. Everyone who's had any contact with Leo Weisse will remember how he was always telling jokes—mostly off-color ones. He had a good sense of humor and an infectious laugh. I remember how he'd always laugh at his own jokes, and just his laugh would make me laugh. I'll miss his jokes and especially his laugh.

We're all very grateful to my dad for many things. He had his diffi-culties, but I want you all to really understand something: he was a very decent human being. His difficulties gave our family a lot of perspective. His death has put our lives in a new perspective. And I'm grateful for this new perspective. We'll grow stronger because of it.

It hurts my family to know we were unable to help my dad at a time when he was in very deep emotional pain. Maybe if we'd had a joke for him it would have helped him with a little perspective. Leo Weisse had many positive qualities. I believe he'd like to be remembered for two of those qualities in particular. First, remember his lightheartedness. He laughed and told jokes and made everyone around him feel more com-fortable. Second, remember his willingness to lend an unconditional hand of assistance. He was a good guy.

Bye, Dad. And thank you.

Again, thank you all for being here and thank you all for your support.

"I'M THE OTHER ONE"

At the memorial service for New York newscaster Roger Grimsby, his longtime coanchor, Bill Beutel, eulogized his friend in a way very typical of the rough-and-tumble humor of the newsroom they inhabited together for decades. At the end, his self-deprecation is a moving tribute to his friend and the fame they shared.

Roger would be pleased to see all of us here tonight. Well, pleased or surprised. And he might ask, "Don't you have anything better to do tonight?"

The answer is no. We are friends and family, and we do not have anything better to do tonight than to celebrate the life and reluctantly accept the death of Roger Grimsby.

Maria. He loved you, and we who are his friends thank you for the joy and love you gave him. And Karen. He loved you. He told me a couple of weeks ago that he was going to visit you soon . . . and that he was looking forward to seeing and talking with you. We thank you, Maria and Karen, and Maria's children, for allowing us to share your loss tonight.

I first met Roger in 1964, more than thirty years ago, at the Republican convention in San Francisco, where [he] was already a legend. He became a legend by doing some of those things that gave ulcers and prematurely gray hair to hapless generations of station managers. He half-heartedly denied many of the stories that contributed to the legend. But the fact that you are here tonight tells me that you believe they are true.

We met in 1964, but our careers did not share a pathway till 1970, when the powers that were at Channel Seven decided to put us together. It was a stroke of genius, and we believed sincerely that we saved the careers of several executives who thought, for example, that Joey Bishop was the answer to Johnny Carson.

We were a success, and we became friends. Friends and competitors. When you sit side by side, night after night, week after week, year after year, it is helpful if you become friends, inevitable that you will become competitors. And Roger Grimsby was a competitor who did not easily give up power and place. Suffice to say, *Eyewitness News* was, and is, a place where you can find a healthy ego if you're in the market for one.

We were a success. We were together for sixteen years. From September 1970 to April 1986. Longer than Huntley-Brinkley. Maybe longer than any other anchor team. Local or network. We succeeded for several reasons. But chief among them was Roger himself. He was a wonderful writer who knew and understood the use and importance of words. Even, and maybe especially, in a visual medium. He was a wonderful writer and a gifted performer.

But most of all, Roger was a newsman. He took great pride in his work in radio. A newscast every day. He wrote it. Loved the process of putting it together. And he felt always that radio newsmen were the real heroes of broadcast journalism because of the purity of their medium. They have only their voices and their words. They work without the help of body language and gesture. Roger worried that the writers and producers and newscasters in radio would be ignored after the merger with Cap Cities. They were his friends. And if you were Roger's friend, he worried about you. And in quiet ways tried to make your days a little easier.

And Roger loved the news itself. He relished his trips to Cape Canaveral for a space launch. To Washington for an inauguration. To South Africa. To the Middle East. To Geneva for a summit meeting. To Vietnam thirty years ago. And then to return to Vietnam on his own two years ago. And unbelievably, he persuaded the management one summer to send him to do a documentary on the problems and enticements of Micronesia. I joked with him about this a couple of months ago, and he stoutly defended his trip to those Pacific paradises. He said there was a story there. He was just ahead of the curve. Maybe a dozen years ahead of the curve.

We have shared so many magic moments over the years. Some of them can be retold. For some of them, you just had to be there.

One day, some years ago, Roger was doing a bit about the Middle East and shuttle diplomacy. He stared into the camera, as was his custom. And he began, "Today Secretary of State . . ." and the prompter got stuck. He kept staring into the prompter, willing it to move. And I leaned into his camera and whispered, "Kissinger. Kissinger."

He told the story of a meeting with Marcos of the Philippines. Marcos agreed to be interviewed, he said, because he had heard that Roger was the highest-paid anchorman in America. I didn't know that.

Nine years ago, Roger left Channel Seven. But the people don't seem to believe it. Even now, when I walk down the street, they wave and say, "Hi, Roger." Or they stop and say, "Hello, Mr. Grimsby." And I say, "Thank you. I'm the other one."

And over the past few days, on the street, in the elevator, in the garage, on the golf course, so many men and women have come up to me and said, "I'm so sorry about your partner."

My partner. What a pain in the neck. What an honor. What a joy. What a chuckle it was to be Roger Grimsby's partner.

CHAPTER TEN

MAKING IT HAPPEN

Among other things, a memorial service or a funeral is a large logistical undertaking, involving as it does notifying and gathering large numbers of people. If you choose to use the services of a funeral home, much of the detail work—placing obituaries, finding an appropriate meeting place, handling seating, parking, checking coats—can be handled for you. If you choose a more personalized service, you will have to attend to those details yourself or with the help of friends. Here are some suggestions for accomplishing the necessary tasks.

GETTING THE WORD OUT

- Find names and addresses.
- Check locations for important documents to see if a notification list has been prepared.
- Check address books and computer files.
- Identify important circles: work, family, former employers, neighborhoods, former neighborhoods, college and high school friends. Set up a telephone tree. Notify one person in each circle and ask him or her to phone as many people as possible.
- Call organizations and ask them to place notices.

- Check E-mail accounts for master mailing lists. Broadcast an E-mail message to friends and colleagues.
- Place obituaries in important newspapers in each place where the deceased spent a meaningful part of her life.

WRITING THE OBITUARY

Obituary writers for metropolitan papers are used to receiving copy in a usable format from funeral homes. If you are going to write and submit the obituary yourself, ask for the format of the local paper and prepare the obituary along those lines. Be sure to include significant biographical details: age, reason for death, closest surviving relatives, place of birth, and important employment or civic contributions. There are generally charges for obituary and funeral notices.

If your friend or relative was of some special importance to the community, a larger obituary may be written in the form of a news story. In most cases, it will be up to you to prepare something that goes beyond the ordinary obituary format—a kind of mini–press release with a photograph—if you wish that sort of obituary. If you can find a résumé or curriculum vitae, it will be very helpful in preparing both the routine obituary and the larger story.

LOGISTICS

Think wedding. If you are planning a special service, the types of help available for weddings can also be appropriate for memorial services. Florists can provide not just the traditional large sprays for the service but also baskets of flowers for a flower communion and bags of petals for scattering. Nearly every town has a place that can supply helium balloons and materials for banners and hangings. The same types of musical groups—from contemporary to classical—can be appropriate for memorial services. With their large selection of pop and contemporary recordings, deejays can possibly save you the time of prowling through music stores looking for selections. If you are holding a large outdoor service, you may have to look for a supplier of chairs or tents.

Here is a checklist of many of the common needs:
- Parking
- Seating (arrange for more seating than you think you will need)
- Space for hanging coats
- Podium for speaker
- Acoustic system (if the meeting place is large)
- Audiovisual equipment (if showing a video or playing recorded music)
- Musicians (if using live music)
- Programs
- Flowers for front of service
- Boutonnieres for ushers
- Table for memorabilia
- Traffic control (if you are expecting many people)

FLOWERS

If you are arranging a memorial service, you need to consider both purchasing flowers to be used at the church, funeral home, or grave site and transporting the flowers that others will send you. Flowers are typically sent to the funeral home, where they are displayed around the casket. Floral arrangements designed specifically for funerals are arranged with such display in mind. Thus, a simple bouquet may be arranged in a basket that can stand on a floor or table. Larger arrangements come with their own stands. The most elaborate displays include gladiolas, chrysanthemums, and roses woven over a form to create shapes such as hearts, crosses, or wreaths. Costs range from about $40 for a small basket to more than $200 for larger standing displays. If the funeral home is arranging transportation of the body from its facility or the church to the cemetery, it will also transport the flowers. Otherwise you must remember that an additional vehicle may be required if the displays are large.

Increasingly, however, families are asking that friends and relatives make contributions to a favorite charity in lieu of giving flowers. Indeed, many include such requests in obituaries and paid death announcements.

HONORARIA

Professional musicians, unless they are close friends of the family and performing as an honor or gift to the family, will need to be paid at prevailing rates. It is also customary to give an honorarium to clergy who officiate in their professional capacity. Depending on local custom, anything from $25 to $100 is appropriate. But what if you are unsure about honoraria—for example, if the clergy is an old family friend? You can always write a check in the clergy's name as a donation to be used for whatever purposes he or she chooses.

THE PROGRAM

A program can be as simple as a mimeographed sheet or as formal as an engraved invitation. It isn't necessary to have a program, of course, but there are many reasons why it's desirable.

If the service is a religious one, it can serve as instruction, helping people who are unfamiliar with the service find their way comfortably through the ceremony. It could also include the words to hymns and prayers. If the service is secular, it will inform people of the order of the service, who is speaking, and what music is being played. For more complicated services, a program is almost a necessity. At the memorial service for several members of the Peninsula Flying Club who were killed in a plane crash, for instance, the program explained how the ashes would be scattered by fellow jumpers, which plane carried the ashes of which club member, and what the order of takeoff was.

Here is a simple format for a basic program:

Name of the deceased

Age

Name and address of the place where the service is to be held

Date and hour of the service

Name of officiant

The order of service:
- Names of speakers
- Prayers or readings
- Hymns or other musical selections
- Instructions about standing or sitting if appropriate

Invitation to any lunch or reception afterward

Picture of the deceased

A program can also be an extension of the service. You might want to include an essay written by a friend or a member of the family, some important writing done by the deceased, a picture, or an appropriate piece of poetry. Here is an example of a more elaborate program that featured a farewell poem by a child:

A folder made out of purple construction paper

Cover: Red crayon scribbles and one silver star by a very young child named Sam

Inscription: "In honor of X, May 21, 1953–July 1, 1988"

Inside the folder on the left side, the child's interpretation of the scribbles, a poem in three parts:

    I. I'm going to make stars for his bad dreams
        I know stars make bad dreams go away
        Does he like an orange?
        That looks like a moon
        And that's an engine part that works on paper clips
        Look what I drawed, it's a snail
        Does he like snails?
   II. How 'bout I draw him a magic dot
        With your magic marker?
        It's growing and growing
        Looks now like an engine for his car.
 III. He needs a heart here
        hearts aren't red, they are pink, silly

look, lots of color
Here, let me put some colors on your thing.
Love, Sam*

FOOD

Many cultures have strong food traditions associated with funerals and memorial services: boiled lamb and rice pilaf for Armenians; an all-vegetarian meal for Buddhists; fish, boiled wheat, and almonds for Greek Orthodox; the stout and whiskey that sometimes make the Irish wake a boisterous affair.

Some of these traditions have strong symbolic associations. Some simply trace back to the need to feed mourners who have traveled long distances to attend the service. In any case, the association of food with funerals and memorial services persists, because food—and gathering around it—fulfills important social needs.

For one thing, food is consoling in its own right. Over and over the people we interviewed spoke of the nice meals they had shared: lox, bagels, and a cold-cut spread at Sheldon Dickstein's funeral in Georgia; fried chicken and cole slaw donated by a local restaurant for the memorial service for the skydivers of the Peninsula Flying Club. Even the preparation of the food was often an important community function, consoling both to the helpers and to those who were helped. Churchwomen and friends cooked the meal that was served in the Presbyterian church hall following the service for J. Alex Fife; graduate students bought and set up the wine and beer that followed the service for their professor, Steve Tudor.

The more relaxed atmosphere of a meal or reception can actually serve as an extension of the service by providing an opportunity for family and friends to console one another and to reminisce together. There is also the very real fact that a funeral or memorial service is, like a wedding, an important social event. It gathers people together who may not have seen each other for years. "They were some of the best family reunions we ever had," said one man of the services held for some elderly

*Madeleine Blais, "I Never Knew Whether I Could Let Go," *The Washington Post*, January 26, 1992, p. W6.

relatives. Particularly where the death was at the end of a long and fulfilled life, there is nothing more natural than for relatives and friends to gather and socialize together, to catch up on life in the face of death.

Unlike a wedding, however, a funeral or memorial service is rarely followed by a large, formal sit-down dinner. Of course, a small group may go to a restaurant for dinner. But usually, a simple buffet suffices. Barring religious objections to liquor, most meals following American services do include wine and beer. But be aware that ethnic traditions may vary considerably. One man recalled a memorial service for a colleague at Radio Free Europe where punch and champagne were served, which shocked colleagues from the Balkan countries. All the people of Anglo-Saxon heritage, on the other hand, walked right up and drank a toast to the deceased.

WHAT CAN FRIENDS DO?

"What can I do to help?"

It's a heartfelt question at a time of tragedy, but too often it's one that leaves unsatisfied both the person offering help and the person to whom help is offered. Unless there is some specific task assigned, the would-be helper is left feeling unneeded, while the bereaved feels overwhelmed. Because planning a funeral or a memorial service is such a labor-intensive activity, that needn't be the case. Here is a list of jobs—both practical and ceremonial—that can be distributed among friends.

PRACTICAL TASKS

Answer the telephone and provide information.
Set up and manage a telephone chain to notify people.
Write letters to distant relatives.
Keep track of flowers and donations for thank-you notes.
Arrange for flowers or other decorations.
Help arrange for a charity to receive donations.
Help find and handle arrangements for a location for the service.
Arrange for food for family members during the week before the
    service.

Arrange for food after the service.

Type and reproduce the program or arrange for printing.

Help set up photographs or a memory table.

Help write the obituary.

Baby-sitting.

Help select people who will deliver eulogies.

Handle the logistics of the service:

- Coats
- Chairs
- Parking
- Lectern
- Public-address system
- Music and a system to play it on
- Musicians
- Fees and honoraria to clergy and professional musicians

Meet relatives and friends at the airport:

- Arrange transportation.
- Arrange accommodations.

HONORARY OR SOCIAL ROLES

Pallbearer

Usher

Speaker

Server at a religious service

Reader

Singer/performer

By thus breaking the task into steps, thinking through the meaning of each task, and enlisting all the help you can, you will find that planning and carrying out a memorial service is nowhere near as overwhelming and emotionally draining as you may have expected. Indeed, after the service has concluded, you will doubtless find, as so many people have, that it was well worth the effort. You, your family, your friends, and the community in which you live will all be grateful for the final opportunity to pay a tribute to the memory of someone you all loved.

CHAPTER ELEVEN

POETRY AND OTHER SHORT READINGS FOR THE SERVICE

Poetry and other short readings can play a very meaningful role in a memorial service. Themes of grief, loss, longing, hope, and the expectation of salvation have been powerfully expressed in poetry for hundreds of years. Many people will find their most profound feelings best expressed in verse. For those who do not want to deliver a eulogy, reading a poem or other short selection can be another way of participating.

We have arranged selections according to theme. For some people, the dominant emotion may be grief; for others, hope. Some of the readings express gratitude; others, regret at not having expressed gratitude. There are moving readings that address the loss of a parent, a spouse, a friend. Some of these readings specifically address the topic of death. Others were composed for other reasons but are nonetheless appropriate. They are drawn from the literature of many different countries, over many centuries.

GRIEF AND LOSS

Strew on her roses, roses,
    And never a spray of yew!
In quiet she reposes,
    Ah, would that I did too!

MATTHEW ARNOLD

I REMEMBER THE BLUE RIVER

The moon has a halo, there will be wind.
The boatmen talk together in the night.
Dawn, a brisk wind fills our sail.
We leave the bank and speed over the white waves.
It is no use for me to be here in the land of Wu.
My dream and my desire are back in Ch'ou.
I dreamt that one day she would come with me
On a trip like this, and now she is only dust.

MEI YAO CH'EN

ON THE DEATH OF HIS WIFE

Since we were first married
Seventeen years have past.
Suddenly I looked up and she was gone.
She said she would never leave me.
My temples are turning white.
What have I to grow old for now?
At death we will be together in the tomb.
Now I am still alive,
And my tears flow without end.

MEI YAO CH'EN

ON HIS DEAD WIFE

Methought I saw my late espoused saint
  Brought to me like Alcestis from the grave,
  Whom Jove's great son to her dead husband gave,
  Rescued from death by force, though pale and faint.
Mine, as whom washed from spot of childbed taint
  Purification in the old Law did save,
  And such as yet once more I trust to have
  Full sight of her in heaven without restraint,
Came vested all in white, pure as her mind.
  Her face was veiled, yet to my fancied sight
  Love, sweetness, goodness, in her person shined
So clear as in no face with more delight.
  But O as to embrace me she inclined,
  I waked, she fled, and day brought back my night.

JOHN MILTON

LUCY (II)

She dwelt among the untrodden ways
  Beside the springs of Dove,
A Maid whom there were none to praise
  And very few to love:

A violet by a mossy stone
  Half hidden from the eye!
—Fair as a star, when only one
  Is shining in the sky.

She lived unknown, and few could know
  When Lucy ceased to be;
But she is in her grave, and, oh,
  The difference to me!

WILLIAM WORDSWORTH

READING THE POEMS OF AN ABSENT FRIEND

Tsu Mei is early dead. Chang Yu
Now is somewhere in the South.
And I, unhappy, am like
A four-horse chariot which
Has lost the horses on right
And left. Their memory, like
A strong enemy, attacks
And overthrows me. The feeble
Swarm of my own thoughts struggles
In vain against the shock. All
Men respect hard work, but in
Leisure and repose they find
Happiness and peace. And me,
What is the matter with me?
Nothing, except that I cannot
Bear the loss of friends.

OU YANG HSIU

It is wrong to sorrow without ceasing.

HOMER

I REMEMBER THE RIVER AT WU SUNG

I remember once, on a journey to the west,
An evening at the mouth of the river, at Wu Sung.
Along the banks a fresh breeze blew against the current.
The pale moon rose between two willow trees.
A single night bird flew far away.
Fishing boats wandered on the river.
And who was with me then?
I weep and think of my dead wife.

MEI YAO CH'EN

SURPRISED BY JOY

Surprised by joy—impatient as the wind
   I turned to share the transport—Oh! with whom
   But thee, deep buried in the silent tomb,
That spot which no vicissitude can find?
Love, faithful love, recalled thee to my mind—
   But how could I forget thee? Through what power,
   Even for the least division of an hour,
Have I been so beguiled as to be blind
To my most grievous loss! That thought's return
   Was the worst pang that sorrow ever bore,
Save one, one only, when I stood forlorn,
   Knowing my heart's best treasure was no more;
That neither present time, nor years unborn
   Could to my sight that heavenly face restore.

WILLIAM WORDSWORTH

Real friends are our greatest joy and our greatest sorrow. It were almost to be wished that all true and faithful friends should expire on the same day.

FRANÇOIS FÉNELON

My life closed twice before its close;
   It yet remains to see
If Immortality unveil
   A third event to me,
So huge, so hopeless to conceive,
   As these that twice befell.
Parting is all we know of heaven,
   And all we need of hell.

EMILY DICKINSON

After great pain, a formal feeling comes—
The Nerves sit ceremonious, like Tombs—
The stiff Heart questions—was it He, that bore,
And Yesterday, or Centuries before?

The Feet, mechanical, go round—
Of Ground, or Air, or Ought—
A Wooden way
Regardless grown,
A Quartz contentment, like a stone—

This is the Hour of Lead—
Remembered, if outlived,
As Freezing persons, recollect the Snow—
First—Chill—then Stupor—then the letting go—

EMILY DICKINSON

Your pain is the breaking of the shell that encloses your understanding.
Even as the stone of the fruit must break, that its heart may stand in the sun, so must you know pain.
And could you keep your heart in wonder at the daily miracles of your life, your pain would not seem less wondrous than your joy;
And you would accept the seasons of your heart, even as you have always accepted the seasons that pass over your fields.
And you would watch with serenity through the winters of your grief.

KAHLIL GIBRAN

When we lose a friend we die a little.

ANONYMOUS

There are not ten people in the world whose deaths would spoil my dinner, but there are one or two whose deaths would break my heart.

THOMAS B. MACAULAY

THE OLD FAMILIAR FACES

I have had playmates, I have had companions,
In my days of childhood, in my joyful school-days,
All, all are gone, the old familiar faces.

I have been laughing, I have been carousing,
Drinking late, sitting late, with my bosom cronies,
All, all are gone, the old familiar faces.

I loved a love once, fairest among women:
Closed are her doors on me, I must not see her—
All, all are gone, the old familiar faces.

I have a friend, a kinder friend has no man,
Like an ingrate, I left my friend abruptly;
Left him, to muse on the old familiar faces.

Ghost-like I paced round the haunts of my childhood,
Earth seemed a desert I was bound to traverse,
Seeking to find the old familiar faces.

Friend of my bosom, thou more than a brother,
Why wert not thou born in my father's dwelling?
So might we talk of the old familiar faces—

How some they have died, and some they have left me,
And some are taken from me; all are departed;
All, all are gone, the old familiar faces.

CHARLES LAMB

ON THE DEATH OF RICHARD WEST

In vain to me the smiling mornings shine,
  And reddening Phoebus lifts his golden fire:
The birds in vain their amorous descant join,
  Or cheerful fields resume their green attire:
These ears, alas! for other notes repine,
  A different object do these eyes require.
My lonely anguish melts no heart but mine;
  And in my breast the imperfect joys expire.
Yet morning smiles the busy race to cheer,
  And new-born pleasure brings to happier men;
The fields to all their wonted tribute bear;
  To warm their little loves the birds complain.
I fruitless mourn to him that cannot hear,
  And weep the more because I weep in vain.

THOMAS GRAY

THE CYCLE OF LIFE

THE PEACE OF WILD THINGS

When despair for the world grows in me
and I wake in the night at the least sound
in fear of what my life and my children's lives may be,
I go and lie down where the wood drake
rests in his beauty on the water, and the great heron feeds.
I come into the peace of wild things
who do not tax their lives with forethought
of grief. I come into the presence of still water.
And I feel above me the day-blind stars
waiting with their light. For a time
I rest in the grace of the world, and am free.

WENDELL BERRY

POEM FOR J.

What she made in her body is broken.
Now she has begun to bear it again.
In the house of her son's death
his life is shining in the windows,
for she has elected to bear him again.
She did not bear him for death,
and she does not. She has taken back
into her body the seed, bitter
and joyous, of the life of a man.

In the house of the dead the windows shine
with life. She mourns, for his life was good.
She is not afraid. She is like a field
where the corn is planted, and like the rain
that waters the field, and like the young corn.
In her sorrow she renews life, in her grief
she prepares the return of joy.

She did not bear him for death, and she does not.
There was a life that went out of her to live
on its own, divided, and now she has taken it back.
She is alight with the sudden new life of death.
Perhaps it is the brightness of the dead one
being born again. Perhaps she is planting him,
like corn, in the living and in the earth.
She has taken back into her flesh,
and made light, the dark seed of her pain.

WENDELL BERRY

Death we can face, but knowing, as some of us do, what is human life,
which of us is it that, without shuddering, should (if consciously we
were summoned) face the hour of birth?

THOMAS DE QUINCEY

MUSÉE DES BEAUX ARTS

About suffering they were never wrong,
The Old Masters: how well they understood
Its human position; how it takes place
While someone else is eating or opening a window or just walking
    dully along;
How, when the aged are reverently, passionately waiting
For the miraculous birth, there always must be
Children who did not specially want it to happen, skating
On a pond at the edge of the wood:
They never forgot
That even the dreadful martyrdom must run its course
Anyhow in a corner, some untidy spot
Where the dogs go on with their doggy life and the torturer's horse
Scratches its innocent behind on a tree.

In Brueghel's *Icarus*, for instance: how everything turns away
Quite leisurely from the disaster; the ploughman may
Have heard the splash, the forsaken cry,
But for him it was not an important failure; the sun shone
As it had to on the white legs disappearing into the green
Water; and the expensive delicate ship that must have seen
Something amazing, a boy falling out of the sky,
Had somewhere to get to and sailed calmly on.

W. H. AUDEN

ETERNITY

He who bends to himself a joy
Does the winged life destroy;
But he who kisses the joy as it flies
Lives in eternity's sunrise.

WILLIAM BLAKE

THE BURNING OF THE LEAVES

Now is the time for the burning of the leaves.
They go to the fire; the nostril pricks with smoke
Wandering slowly into a weeping mist.
Brittle and blotched, ragged and rotten sheaves!
A flame seizes the smouldering ruin and bites
On stubborn stalks that crackle as they resist.

The last hollyhock's fallen tower is dust;
All the spices of June are a bitter reek,
All the extravagant riches spent and mean.
All burns! The reddest rose is a ghost;
Sparks whirl up, to expire in the midst: the wild
Fingers of fire are making corruption clean.

Now is the time for stripping the spirit bare,
Time for the burning of days ended and done,
Idle solace of things that have gone before:
Rootless hope and fruitless desire are there;
Let them go to the fire, with never a look behind.
The world that was ours is a world that is ours no more.

They will come again, the leaf and the flower, to arise
From squalor of rottenness into the old splendour,
And magical scents to a wondering memory bring;
The same glory, to shine upon different eyes.
Earth cares for her own ruins, naught for ours.
Nothing is certain, only the certain spring.

LAURENCE BINYON

If thou grievest for the dead, mourn also for those who are born into the world; for as the one thing is of nature, so is the other too of nature.

ST. JOHN CHRYSOSTOM

SONNET TO MY MOTHER

Most near, most dear, most loved and most far,
Under the window where I often found her
Sitting as huge as Asia, seismic with laughter,
Gin and chicken helpless in her Irish hand,
Irresistible as Rabelais but most tender for
The lame dogs and hurt birds that surround her, —
She is a procession no one can follow after
But be like a little dog following a brass band.
She will not glance up at the bomber or condescend
To drop her gin and scuttle to a cellar,
But lean on the mahogany table like a mountain
Whom only faith can move, and so I send
O all my faith and all my love to tell her
That she will move from mourning into morning.

GEORGE BARKER

THE DESPOT'S DESPOT

VITAE SUMMA BREVIS SPEM NOS VETAT INCOHARE LONGAM

They are not long, the weeping and the laughter,
    Love and desire and hate;
I think they have no portion in us after
    We pass the gate.

They are not long, the days of wine and roses:
    Out of a misty dream
Our path emerges for a while, then closes
    Within a dream.

ERNEST DOWSON

No man at all can be living forever, and we must be satisfied.

JOHN M. SYNGE

A SONG OF LIVING

Because I have loved life, I shall have no sorrow to die.
I have sent up my gladness on wings, to be lost in the blue of the sky.
I have run and leaped with the rain, I have taken the wind to my
    breast.
My cheek like a drowsy child to the face of the earth I have pressed.
Because I have loved life, I shall have no sorrow to die.
I have kissed young Love on the lips, I have heard his song to the end.
I have struck my hand like a seal in the loyal hand of a friend.
I have known the peace of heaven, the comfort of work done well.
I have longed for death in the darkness and risen alive out of hell.
Because I have loved life, I shall have no sorrow to die.
I give a share of my soul to the world where my course is run.
I know that another shall finish the task I must leave undone.
I know that no flower, no flint was in vain on the path I trod.
As one looks on a face through a window, through life I have looked
    on God.
Because I have loved life, I shall have no sorrow to die.

AMELIA JOSEPHINE BURR

Has any one supposed it lucky to be born?
I hasten to inform him or her it is just as lucky to die, and I know it.

I pass death with the dying, and birth with the new-washed babe,
    and am not contained between my hat and boots,
And peruse manifold objects, no two alike, and every one good,
The earth good, and the stars good, and their adjuncts all good.

I am not an earth nor an adjunct of an earth,
I am the mate and companion of people, all just as immortal and
        fathomless as myself,
They do not know how immortal, but I know.

WALT WHITMAN

Yet the timeless in you is aware of life's timelessness,

And knows that yesterday is but today's memory and tomorrow is today's dream.

And that that which sings and contemplates in you is still dwelling within the bounds of that first moment which scattered the stars into space.

Who among you does not feel that his power to love is boundless?

And yet who does not feel that very love, though boundless, encompassed within the centre of his being, and moving not from love thought to love thought, nor from love deeds to other love deeds?

And is not time even as love is, undivided and spaceless?

KAHLIL GIBRAN

She died in beauty,—like a rose
 Blown from its parent stem;
She died in beauty,—like a pearl
 Dropped from some diadem.

She died in beauty,—like a lay
 Along a moonlit lake;
She died in beauty,—like the song
 Of birds amid the brake.

She died in beauty,—like the snow
 On flowers dissolved away;
She died in beauty,—like a star
 Lost on the brow of day.

She lives in glory,—like night's gems
 Set round the silver moon;
She lives in glory,—like the sun
 Amid the blue of June.

CHARLES DOYNE SILLERY

You would know the secret of death,

But how shall you find it unless you seek it in the heart of life?

The owl whose night-bound eyes are blind unto the day cannot unveil the mystery of light.

If you would indeed behold the spirit of death, open your heart wide unto the body of life.

For life and death are one, even as the river and the sea are one.

KAHLIL GIBRAN

What, I pray you, is dying? Just what it is to put off a garment. For the body is about the soul as a garment; and after laying this aside for a short time by means of death, we shall resume it again with the more splendor.

ST. JOHN CHRYSOSTOM

ON THE BEACH AT NIGHT

Weep not, child,

Weep not, my darling,

With these kisses let me remove your tears,

The ravening clouds shall not long be victorious,

They shall not long possess the sky, they devour the stars only in
    apparition,

Jupiter shall emerge, be patient, watch again another night, the
    Pleiades shall emerge,

They are immortal, all those stars both silvery and golden shall shine
    out again,

The great stars and the little ones shall shine out again, they endure.

The vast immortal suns and the long-enduring pensive moons shall
    again shine.

WALT WHITMAN

LUCY (V)

A slumber did my spirit seal;
   I had no human fears:
She seemed a thing that could not feel
   The touch of earthly years.

No motion has she now, no force;
   She neither hears nor sees;
Rolled round in earth's diurnal course,
   With rocks, and stones, and trees.

WILLIAM WORDSWORTH

I too pass from the night,
I stay awhile away O night, but I return to you again and love you.

Why should I be afraid to trust myself to you?
I am not afraid, I have been well brought forward by you,
I love the rich running day, but I do not desert her in whom I lay so long.
I know not how I came of you, and I know not where I go with you—
   but I know I came well and shall go well.

I will stop only a time with the night, and rise betimes,
I will duly pass the day O my mother and duly return to you.

WALT WHITMAN

LOVE IS FOREVER

I love thee with a love I seemed to lose
With my lost saints,—I love thee with the breath,
Smiles, tears, of all my life!—and, if God choose,
I shall but love thee better after death.

ELIZABETH BARRETT BROWNING

As fair art thou, my bonny lass,
   So deep in luve am I;
And I will luve thee still, my dear,
   Till a' the seas gang dry.

Till a' the seas gang dry, my dear,
   And the rocks melt wi' the sun;
I will luve thee still, my dear,
   While the sands o' life shall run.

ROBERT BURNS

Many waters cannot quench love, neither can the floods drown it.

SONG OF SOLOMON, VIII

AN EPITAPH UPON HUSBAND AND WIFE
WHO DIED AND WERE BURIED TOGETHER

To these whom death again did wed
This grave's their second marriage-bed.
For though the hand of Fate could force
'Twixt soul and body a divorce,
It could not sever man and wife,
Because they both lived but one life.
Peace, good reader, do not weep;
Peace, the lovers are asleep.
They, sweet turtles, folded lie
In the last knot that love could tie.
Let them sleep, let them sleep on,
Till this stormy night be gone,
And the eternal morrow dawn;
Then the curtains will be drawn,
And they wake into a light
Whose day shall never die in night.

RICHARD CRASHAW

O pale, pale now, those rosy lips,
   I aft hae kissed sae fondly,
And closed for aye the sparkling glance
   That dwelt on me sae kindly;

And mouldering now in silent dust
   That heart that loved me dearly,
And still within my bosom's core
   Shall live my Highland Mary.

ROBERT BURNS

THE DEAD LIVE ON

IN BROAD DAYLIGHT I DREAM OF MY DEAD WIFE

Who says that the dead do not think of us?
Whenever I travel, she goes with me.
She was uneasy when I was on a journey.
She always wanted to accompany me.
While I dream, everything is as it used to be.
When I wake up, I am stabbed with sorrow.
The living are often parted and never meet again.
The dead are together as pure souls.

MEI YAO CH'EN

HALLOWED GROUND

But strew his ashes to the wind
Whose sword or voice has served mankind,—
And is he dead, whose glorious mind
   Lifts thine on high?—
To live in hearts we leave behind
   Is not to die.

THOMAS CAMPBELL

A remembrance is moving
down the long memory, disturbing
the dry leaves with its delicate feet.

—Behind, the house is empty.
On ahead, highways
going on to other places, solitary highways,
stretched out.
And the rain is like weeping eyes,
as if the eternal moment were going blind—.

Even though the house is quiet and shut,
even though I am not in it, I am in it.
And . . . good-bye, you who are walking
without turning your head!

JUAN RAMÓN JIMÉNEZ

HE IS NOT DEAD

I cannot say, and I will not say
That he is dead. He is just away.
With a cheery smile, and a wave of the hand,
He has wandered into an unknown land
And left us dreaming how very fair
It needs must be, since he lingers there.
And you—oh, you, who the wildest yearn
For an old-time step, and the glad return,
Think of him faring on, as dear
In the love of There as the love of Here.
Think of him still as the same. I say,
He is not dead—he is just away.

JAMES WHITCOMB RILEY

in populated air
our ancestors continue.
I have seen them.
I have heard
their shimmering voices
singing.

LUCILLE CLIFTON

FOREVER

Those we love truly never die,
Though year by year the sad memorial wreath,
A ring and flowers, types of life and death,
    Are laid upon their graves.

    For death the pure life saves,
And life all pure is love; and love can reach
From heaven to earth, and nobler lessons teach
    Than those by mortals read.

    Well blest is he who has a dear one dead:
A friend he has whose face will never change —
A dear communion that will not grow strange;
    The anchor of a love is death.

    The blessed sweetness of a loving breath
Will reach our cheek all fresh through weary years.
For her who died long since, ah! waste not tears,
    She's thine unto the end.

    Thank God for one dear friend,
With face still radiant with the light of truth,
Whose love comes laden with the scent of youth,
    Through twenty years of death.

JOHN BOYLE O'REILLY

I am not I.
       I am this one
walking beside me whom I do not see,
whom at times I manage to visit,
and whom at other times I forget;
who remains calm and silent while I talk,
and forgives, gently, when I hate,
who walks where I am not,
who will remain standing when I die.

JUAN RAMÓN JIMÉNEZ

The life of the dead consists in being present in the minds of the living.

CICERO

If we treat the dead as if they were wholly dead it shows want of affection; if we treat them as wholly alive it shows want of sense. Neither should be done.

CONFUCIUS

Ha! Dead! Impossible! It cannot be!
I'd not believe it though himself should swear it.

HENRY CAREY

AFTERWARD

There is no vacant chair. To love is still
    To have. Nearer to memory than to eye.
And dearer yet to anguish than to comfort, will
    We hold by our love, that shall not die.

ELIZABETH STUART PHELPS WARD

What do you think has become of the young and old men?
And what do you think has become of the women and children?

They are alive and well somewhere,
The smallest sprout shows there is really no death,
And if ever there was it led forward life, and does not wait at the
    end to arrest it,
And ceased the moment life appeared.

All goes onward and outward—and nothing collapses,
And to die is different from what any one suppose, and luckier.

WALT WHITMAN

DEATH IS A JOURNEY

SEALED ORDERS

We bear sealed orders o'er Life's weltered sea,
    Our haven dim and far;
We can but man the helm right cheerily,
    Steer by the Brightest star,

And hope that when at last the Great Command
    Is read, we then may hear
Our anchor song, and see the longed-for land
    Lie, known and very near.

RICHARD BURTON

'Tis but a tent where takes his one-day's rest
A sultan to the realm of death addrest;
    The sultan rises, and the dark ferrash
Strikes, and prepares it for another guest.

OMAR KHAYYAM

Some time at eve when the tide is low,
  I shall slip my mooring and sail away,
With no response to the friendly hail
  Of kindred craft in the busy bay.
In the silent hush of the twilight pale,
  When the night stoops down to embrace the day,
And the voices call in the waters' flow—
Some time at eve when the tide is low,
  I shall slip my mooring and sail away.

Through the purpling shadows that darkly trail
  O'er the ebbing tide of the Unknown Sea,
I shall fare me away, with a dip of sail
And a ripple of waters to tell the tale
  Of a lonely voyager, sailing away
  To the Mystic Isles where at anchor lay
The crafts of those who have sailed before
O'er the Unknown Sea to the Unseen Shore.

A few who have watched me sail away
Will miss my craft from the busy bay;
  Some friendly barks that were anchored near,
  Some loving souls that my heart held dear,
  In silent sorrow will drop a tear—
But I shall have peacefully furled my sail
In moorings sheltered from storm of Gale,
  And greeted the friends who have sailed before
  O'er the Unknown Sea to the Unseen Shore.

ELIZABETH CLARK HARDY

No one knows but that death is the greatest of all good to man; yet men fear it, as if they well knew that it is the greatest of evils. Is not this the more reprehensible ignorance, to think that one knows what one does not know?

SOCRATES

AWAY!

Now I out walking
The world desert,
And my shoe and my stocking
Do me no hurt.

I leave behind
good friends in town.
Let them get well-wined
And go lie down.

Don't think I leave
For the outer dark
Like Adam and Eve
Put out of the Park.

Forget the myth.
There is no one I
Am put out with
Or put out by.

Unless I'm wrong
I but obey
The urge of a song:
"I'm—bound—away!"

And I may return
If dissatisfied
With what I learn
From having died.

ROBERT FROST

from "SONGS IN ABSENCE"

Where lies the land to which the ship would go?
Far, far ahead, is all her seamen know.
And where the land she travels from? Away,
Far, far behind, is all that they can say.

On sunny noons upon the deck's smooth face,
Linked arm in arm, how pleasant here to pace;
Or, o'er the stern reclining, watch below
The foaming wake far widening as we go.

On stormy nights, when wild north-westers rave,
How proud a thing to fight with wind and wave!
The dripping sailor on the reeling mast
Exults to bear, and scorn to wish it past.

Where lies the land to which the ship would go?
Far, far ahead, is all her seamen know.
And where the land she travels from? Away,
Far, far behind, is all that they can say.

ARTHUR HUGH CLOUGH

There are no graves here.
These mountains and plains are a cradle and a stepping-stone.
Whenever you pass by the field where you have laid your ancestors
look well thereupon, and you shall see yourselves and your children
dancing hand in hand.
Verily you often make merry without knowing.

KAHLIL GIBRAN

The body of a man is not a home but an inn—and that only briefly.
SENECA

Human existence is girt round with mystery: the narrow region of our experience is a small island in the midst of a boundless sea. To add to the mystery, the domain of our earthly existence is not only an island of infinite space, but also in infinite time. The past and the future are alike shrouded from us: we neither know the origin of anything which is, nor its final destination.

JOHN STUART MILL

DEATH IS A DOOR

Death is only an old door
Set in a garden wall;
On gentle hinges it gives, at dusk
When the thrushes call.

Along the lintel are green leaves,
Beyond the light lies still;
Very willing and weary feet
Go over that sill.

There is nothing to trouble any heart;
Nothing to hurt at all.
Death is only a quiet door
In an old wall.

NANCY BYRD TURNER

CROSSING THE BAR

Sunset and evening star,
　　And one clear call for me!
And may there be no moaning of the bar,
　　When I put out to sea,

But such a tide as moving seems asleep,
　　Too full for sound and foam,

When that which drew from out the boundless deep
   Turns again home.

Twilight and evening bell,
   And after that the dark!
And may there be no sadness of farewell,
   When I embark;

For though from out our bourne of Time and Place
   The flood may bear me far,
I hope to see my Pilot face to face,
   When I have crossed the bar.

ALFRED, LORD TENNYSON

DEATH BRINGS PEACE

REQUIEM

Under the wide and starry sky
Dig the grave and let me lie.
Glad did I live and gladly die,
   And I laid me down with a will.

This be the verse you grave for me:
Here he lies where he longed to be;
Home is the sailor, home from the sea,
   And the hunter home from the hill.

ROBERT LOUIS STEVENSON

Flow gently, sweet Afton, among thy green braes;
Flow gently, I'll sing thee a song in thy praise;
My Mary's asleep by thy murmuring stream.
Flow gently, sweet Afton, disturb not her dream.

ROBERT BURNS

Duncan is in his grave;
After life's fitful fever he sleeps well;
Treason has done his worst: nor steel, nor poison,
Malice domestic, foreign levy, nothing
Can touch him further.

WILLIAM SHAKESPEARE

He has outsoared the shadow of our night;
Envy and calumny and hate and pain,
And that unrest which men miscall delight
Can touch him not and torture not again.

PERCY BYSSHE SHELLEY

And I call to mankind, Be not curious about God,
For I who am curious about each am not curious about God,
No array of terms can say how much I am at peace about God and
   about death.

WALT WHITMAN

GUILT

TABLEAU VIVANT

They think it's easy to be dead, those
who walk the pathway here in stylish shoes,
portable radios strapped to their arms,
selling the world's perishables, even
love songs. They think you just lie down
into dreams you will never tell anyone.
They don't know we still have plans, a yen
for romance, and miss things like hats
and casseroles.

As for dreams, we take up where the living
leave off. We like especially those
in which the dreamer is about to
fall over a cliff or from a bridge that
is falling too. We're only too glad
to look down on the river gorge enlarging
under a body's sudden weight, to have the ground
rushing up instead of this slow
caving in. We thrive on living out
the last precious memories of someone escaped
back into the morning light.

Occasionally there's a message saying they want
one of us back, someone out there
feeling guilt about a word or deed
that seems worse because we took it as
a living harm, then died
with it, quietly. But we know a lot about
forgiveness and we always make these trips with
a certain missionary zeal. We get back
into our old sad clothes. We stand again
at the parting, full of wronged tenderness and
needing a shave or a hairdo. We tell them
things are okay, not to waste their lives
in remorse, we never held it
against them, so much happens that one means.

But sometimes one of us gets stubborn, thinks
of evening the score. We leave them calling
after us, Sorry, Sorry, Sorry, and we don't
look back.

TESS GALLAGHER

THE VIRTUES OF THE DEAD

IN MEMORY OF W. B. YEATS
(D. JAN. 1939)

I

He disappeared in the dead of winter:
The brooks were frozen, the airports almost deserted,
And snow disfigured the public statues;
The mercury sank in the mouth of the dying day.
O all the instruments agree
The day of his death was a dark cold day.

Far from his illness
The wolves ran on through the evergreen forests,
The peasant river was untempted by the fashionable quays;
By mourning tongues
The death of the poet was kept from his poems.

But for him it was his last afternoon as himself,
An afternoon of nurses and rumours;
The provinces of his body revolted,
The squares of his mind were empty,
Silence invaded the suburbs,
The current of his feeling failed: he became his admirers.

Now he is scattered among a hundred cities
And wholly given over to unfamiliar affections;
To find his happiness in another kind of wood
And be punished under a foreign code of conscience.
The words of a dead man
Are modified in the guts of the living.

But in the importance and noise of tomorrow
When the brokers are roaring like beasts on the floor of the Bourse,

And the poor have the sufferings to which they are fairly accustomed,
And each in the cell of himself is almost convinced of his freedom;
A few thousand will think of this day
As one thinks of a day when one did something slightly unusual.
O all the instruments agree
The day of his death was a dark cold day.

II

You were silly like us: your gift survived it all;
The parish of rich women, physical decay,
Yourself; mad Ireland hurt you into poetry.
Now Ireland has her madness and her weather still,
For poetry makes nothing happen: it survives
In the valley of its saying where executives
Would never want to tamper; it flows south
From ranches of isolation and the busy griefs,
Raw towns that we believe and die in; it survives,
A way of happening, a mouth.

W. H. AUDEN

AN EPITAPH INTENDED FOR HIMSELF

Like thee I once have stemmed the sea of life,
    Like thee have languished after empty joys,
Like thee have labored in the stormy strife,
    Been grieved for trifles, and amused with toys.

Forget my frailties; thou art also frail:
    Forgive my lapses; for thyself may'st fall
Nor read unmoved my artless tender tale—
    I was a friend, O man, to thee, to all.

JAMES BEATTIE

That individuals have soared above the plane of their race is scarcely to
be questioned; but, in looking back through history for traces of
their existence we should pass over all biographies of "the good and
the great," while we search carefully the slight records of wretches
who died in prison, in Bedlam, or upon the gallows.

EDGAR ALLAN POE

THE WITNESS

In a stable that stands almost within the shadow of the new stone church a
gray-eyed, gray-bearded man, stretched out amid the odor of the animals,
humbly seeks death as one seeks for sleep. The day, faithful to vast secret
laws, little by little shifts and mingles the shadows in the humble nook. Outside are the plowed fields and a deep ditch clogged with dead leaves and an
occasional wolf track in the black earth at the edge of the forest. The man
sleeps and dreams, forgotten. The Angelus awakens him. By now the
sound of the bells is one of the habits of evening in the kingdoms of Eng-
land. But this man, as a child, saw the face of Woden, the holy dread and
exultation, the rude wooden idol weighed down with Roman coins and
heavy vestments, the sacrifice of horses, dogs, and prisoners. Before dawn
he will die, and in him will die, never to return, the last eye-witness of those
pagan rites; the world will be a little poorer when this Saxon dies.

Events far-reaching enough to people all space, whose end is nonetheless tolled when one man dies, may cause us wonder. But something, or
an infinite number of things, dies in every death, unless the universe is
possessed of a memory, as the theosophists have supposed.

In the course of time there was a day that closed the last eyes to see
Christ. The battle of Junin and the love of Helen each died with the
death of some one man. What will die with me when I die, what pitiful
or perishable form will the world lose? The voice of Macedonio Fer-
nández? The image of a roan horse on the vacant lot at Serrano and
Charcas? A bar of sulphur in the drawer of a mahogany desk?

JORGE LUIS BORGES

It matters not how a man dies, but how he lives. The act of dying is of no importance, it lasts so short a time.

SAMUEL JOHNSON

> Lives of great men all remind us
> We can make our lives sublime,
> And, departing, leave behind us
> Footprints on the sands of time.
>
> HENRY WADSWORTH LONGFELLOW

A good death does honor to a whole life.

FRANCESCO PETRARCH

THOSE WINTER SUNDAYS

Sundays too my father got up early
and put his clothes on in the blueblack cold,
then with cracked hands that ached
from labor in the weekday weather made
banked fires blaze. No one ever thanked him.

I'd wake and hear the cold splintering, breaking.
When the rooms were warm, he'd call,
and slowly I would rise and dress,
fearing the chronic angers of that house,

Speaking indifferently to him,
who had driven out the cold
and polished my good shoes as well.
What did I know, what did I know
of love's austere and lonely offices?

ROBERT HAYDEN

I knew a man—he was a common farmer—he was the father of
   five sons—and in them were the fathers of sons—and in them
   were the fathers of sons.

This man was a wonderful vigor and calmness and beauty of person,
The shape of his head, the richness and breadth of his manners, the
   pale yellow and white of his hair and beard, the immeasurable
   meaning of his black eyes.
These I used to go and visit him to see—he was wise also,
   massive clean bearded tan-faced and handsome,
They and his daughters loved him—all who saw him loved him—
   they did not love him by allowance—they loved him with personal love,
He drank water only—the blood showed like scarlet through the
   clear-brown skin of his face,
He was a frequent gunner and fisher—he sailed his boat himself—he
   had a fine one presented to him by a ship-joiner—he had fowling-
   pieces, presented to him by men that loved him,
When he went with his five sons and many grand-sons to hunt or fish
   you would pick him out as the most beautiful and vigorous of the gang,
You would wish long and long to be with him—you would wish to
   sit by him in the boat that you and he might touch each other.

                    WALT WHITMAN

A FUNERAL ELEGY

   For when the world lies wintered in the storms
   Of fearful consummation, and lays down
   Th' unsteady change of his fantastic forms,
   Expecting ever to be overthrown;
   When the proud height of much affected sin
   Shall ripen to a head, and in that pride
   End in the miseries it did begin
   And fall amidst the glory of his tide;
   Then in a book where every work is writ
   Shall this man's actions be revealed, to show

The gainful fruit of well-employed wit,
Which paid to heaven the debt that it did owe.
Here shall be reckoned up the constant faith,
Never untrue, where once he love professed;
Which is a miracle in men, one saith,
Long sought though rarely found, and he is best
  Who can make friendship, in those times of change,
  Admired more for being firm than strange.

WILLIAM SHAKESPEARE

MILITARY

FOR THE FALLEN
(1914)

They went with songs to the battle, they were young,
Straight of limb, true of eye, steady and aglow.
They were staunch to the end against odds uncounted,
They fell with their faces to the foe.

They shall grow not old, as we that are left grow old:
Age shall not weary them, nor the years condemn.
At the going down of the sun and in the morning
We will remember them.

LAURENCE BINYON

IN MEMORIAM (EASTER, 1915)

The flowers left thick at nightfall in the wood
This Eastertide call into mind the men,
Now far from home, who, with their sweethearts, should
Have gathered them and will do never again.

EDWARD THOMAS

AN IRISH AIRMAN FORESEES HIS DEATH

I know that I shall meet my fate
Somewhere among the clouds above;
Those that I fight I do not hate,
Those that I guard I do not love;
My country is Kiltartan Cross,
My countrymen Kiltartan's poor,
No likely end could bring them loss
Or leave them happier than before.
Nor law, nor duty bade me fight,
Nor public men, nor cheering crowds,
A lonely impulse of delight
Drove to this tumult in the clouds;
I balanced all, brought all to mind,
The years to come seemed waste of breath,
A waste of breath the years behind
In balance with this life, this death.

WILLIAM BUTLER YEATS

A BETTER WORLD

THE DEATH-BED

We watched her breathing through the night,
Her breathing soft and low,
As in her breast the wave of life
Kept heaving to and fro!

So silently we seemed to speak—
So slowly moved about!
As we had lent her half our powers
To eke her living out!

Our very hopes belied our fears
Our fears our hopes belied—
We thought her dying when she slept,
And sleeping when she died!

For when the morn came dim and sad—
And chill with early showers,
Her quiet eyelids closed—she had
Another morn than ours!

THOMAS HOOD

What is to come we know not. But we know
That what has been was good—was good to show,
Better to hide, and best of all to bear.
We are the masters of the days that were:
We have lived, we have loved, we have suffered . . .
   even so.

Shall we not take the ebb who had the flow?
Life was our friend. Now if it be our foe—
Dear, though it spoil and break us!—need we care
   What is to come?

Let the great winds their worst and wildest blow,
Or the gold weather round us mellow slow
We have fulfilled ourselves, and we can dare,
And we can conquer, though we may not share
In the rich quiet of the after-glow
   What is to come.

WILLIAM ERNEST HENLEY

FRIENDS

We have slept together,
Rose at an instant, learn'd, play'd, eat together;
And wheresoe'er we went, like Juno's swans,
Still we went coupled and inseparable.

WILLIAM SHAKESPEARE

DELIA ELENA SAN MARCO

We said goodbye at the corner of Eleventh. From the other sidewalk I turned to look back; you too had turned, and you waved goodbye to me.

A river of vehicles and people was flowing between us. It was five o'clock on an ordinary afternoon. How was I to know that that river was Acheron the doleful, the insuperable?

We did not see each other again, and a year later you were dead.

And now I seek out that memory and look at it, and I think it was false, and that behind that trivial farewell was infinite separation.

Last night I stayed in after dinner and reread, in order to understand these things, the last teaching Plato put in his master's mouth. I read that the soul may escape when the flesh dies.

And now I do not know whether the truth is in the ominous subsequent interpretation, or in the unsuspecting farewell.

For if souls do not die, it is right that we should not make much of saying goodbye.

To say goodbye to each other is to deny separation. It is like saying "today we play at separating, but we will see each other tomorrow." Man invented farewells because he somehow knows he is immortal, even though he may seem gratuitous and ephemeral.

Sometime, Delia, we will take up again—beside what river?—this uncertain dialogue, and we will ask each other if ever, in a city lost on a plain, we were Borges and Delia.

JORGE LUIS BORGES

HERACLITUS

They told me, Heraclitus, they told me you were dead,
They brought me bitter news to hear and bitter tears to shed
I wept as I remembered how often you and I
Had tired the sun with talking and sent him down the sky.

And now that thou art lying, my dear old Carian guest
A handful of gray ashes, long, long ago at rest,
Still are they pleasant voices, they nightingales, awake;
For Death, he taketh all away, but them he cannot take.

WILLIAM JOHNSON-CORY

Green be the turf above thee,
   Friend of my better days!
None knew thee but to love thee,
   Nor named thee but to praise.

FITZ-GREENE HALLECK

MEMORY

AULD LANG SYNE

Should auld acquaintance be forgot,
   And never brought to min'?
Should auld acquaintance be forgot,
   And auld lang syne?

For auld lang syne, my dear,
   For auld lang syne,
We'll tak a cup o' kindness yet,
   For auld lang syne.

ROBERT BURNS

THE GOING

Why did you give no hint that night
That quickly after the morrow's dawn,
And calmly, as if indifferent quite,
You would close your term here, up and be gone
    Where I could not follow
    With wing of swallow
To gain one glimpse of you ever anon!

    Never to bid good-bye,
    Or lip me the softest call,
Or utter a wish for a word, while I
Saw morning harden upon the wall,
    Unmoved, unknowing
    That your great going
Had place that moment, and altered all.

Why do you make me leave the house
And think for a breath it is you I see
At the end of the alley of bending boughs
Where so often at dusk you used to be;
    Till in darkening dankness
    The yawning blankness
Of the perspective sickens me!

    You were she who abode
    By those red-veined rocks far West,
You were the swan-necked one who rode
Along the beetling Beeny Crest,
    And, reining nigh me,
    Would muse and eye me,
While Life unrolled us its very best.

Why, then, latterly did we not speak,
Did we not think of those days long dead,

And ere your vanishing strive to seek
That time's renewal? We might have said,
  "In this bright spring weather
  We'll visit together
Those places that once we visited."

  Well, well! All's past amend,
   Unchangeable. It must go.
I seem but a dead man held on end
To sink down soon. . . . O you could not know
  That such swift fleeing
  No soul foreseeing—
Not even I—would undo me so!

THOMAS HARDY

NO FUNERAL GLOOM

No funeral gloom, my dears, when I am gone,
Corpse-gazing, tears, black raiment, graveyard grimness.
Think of me as withdrawn into the dimness,
Yours still, you mine.
Remember all the best of our past moments and forget the rest,
And so to where I wait come gently on.

ELLEN TERRY

THE GLORY OF GOD

  A voice in the wind I do not know;
  A meaning on the face of the high hills
  Whose utterance I cannot comprehend.
  A something is behind them: that is God.

GEORGE MACDONALD

God's in His Heaven—
All's right with the world.
ROBERT BROWNING

Glory be to God for dappled things—
  For skies of couple-colour as a brinded cow;
    For rose-moles all in stipple upon trout that swim;
Fresh-firecoal chestnut-falls; finches' wings;
  Landscape plotted and pieced-fold, fallow, and plough;
    And all trades, their gear and tackle and trim.

All things counter, original, spare, strange;
  Whatever is fickle, freckled (who knows how?)
    With swift, slow; sweet, sour; adazzle, dim;
He fathers-forth whose beauty is past change:
        Praise him.
GERARD MANLEY HOPKINS

As kingfishers catch fire, dragonflies draw flame;
  As tumbled over rim in roundy wells
  Stones ring; like each tucked string tells, each hung bell's
Bow swung finds tongue to fling out broad its name;
Each mortal thing does one thing and the same:
  Deals out that being indoors each one dwells;
  Selves—goes itself; myself it speaks and spells,
Crying What I do is me: for that I came.

I say more: the just man justices;
  Keeps grace: that keeps all his goings graces;
Acts in God's eye what in God's eye he is—
  Christ. For Christ plays in ten thousand places,
Lovely in limbs, and lovely in eyes not his
  To the father through the features of men's faces.
GERARD MANLEY HOPKINS

He prayeth best who loveth best
All things both great and small;
For the dear God who loveth us,
He made and loveth all.

SAMUEL TAYLOR COLERIDGE

VANQUISHING DEATH

Death, be not proud, though some have callèd thee
  Mighty and dreadful, for thou art not so;
For those whom thou think'st thou dost overthrow
Die not, poor Death; nor yet canst thou kill me.
From Rest and Sleep, which but thy pictures be,
Much pleasure; then from thee much more must flow,
And soonest our best men with thee do go,
Rest of their bones and soul's delivery.
Thou'rt slave to fate, chance, kings, and desperate men,
And dost with poison, war, and sickness dwell,
And poppy or charms can make us sleep as well
And better than thy stroke; why swell'st thou then?
  One short sleep past, we wake eternally,
  And death shall be no more: Death, thou shalt die.

JOHN DONNE

Hark! they whisper; angels say,
Sister Spirit, come away!
What is this absorbs me quite,
Steals my senses, shuts my sight,
Drowns my spirits, draws my breath?
Tell me, my soul, can this be death?

The world recedes; it disappears!
Heaven opens on my eyes; my ears

With sounds seraphic ring!
Lend, lend your wings! I mount! I fly!
O Grave! where is thy victory?
O Death! where is thy sting?
ALEXANDER POPE

SONNET 146

Poor soul, the centre of my sinful earth,
Foiled by these rebel powers that thee array,
Why dost thou pine within, and suffer dearth,
Painting thy outward walls so costly gay?
Why so large cost, having so short a lease,
Dost thou upon thy fading mansion spend?
Shall worms, inheritors of this excess,
Eat up thy charge? Is this thy body's end?
Then, soul, live thou upon thy servant's loss,
And let that pine to aggravate thy store;
Buy terms divine in selling hours of dross;
Within be fed, without be rich no more:
    So shalt thou feed on Death, that feeds on men,
    And, Death once dead, there's no more dying then.
WILLIAM SHAKESPEARE

CELEBRATING LIFE

FINAL SOLILOQUY OF THE INTERIOR PARAMOUR

Light the first light of evening, as in a room
In which we rest and, for small reason, think
The world imagined is the ultimate good.

This is, therefore, the intensest rendezvous.
It is in that thought that we collect ourselves,
Out of all the indifferences, into one thing:

Within a single thing, a single shawl
Wrapped tightly round us, since we are poor, a warmth,
A light, a power, the miraculous influence.

Here, now, we forget each other and ourselves.
We feel the obscurity of an order, a whole,
A knowledge, that which arranged the rendezvous,

Within its vital boundary, in the mind.
We say God and the imagination are one . . .
How high that highest candle lights the dark.

Out of this same light, out of the central mind,
We make a dwelling in the evening air,
In which being there together is enough.

WALLACE STEVENS

SONNET 73

That time of year thou mayst in me behold
When yellow leaves, or none, or few, do hang
Upon those boughs which shake against the cold,
Bare ruined choirs, where late the sweet birds sang.
In me thou seest the twilight of such day
As after sunset fadeth in the west;
Which by and by black night doth take away,
Death's second self, that seals up all in rest.
In me thou seest the flowing of such fire,
That on the ashes of his youth doth lie,
As the death-bed whereon it must expire,
Consumed with that which it was nourished by.
  This thou perceiv'st, which makes thy love more strong,
  To love that well which thou must leave ere long.

WILLIAM SHAKESPEARE

Why shed tears that thou must die? For if thy past life has been one of enjoyment, and if all thy pleasures have not passed through thy mind, as through a sieve, and vanished, leaving not a rack behind, why then dost thou not, like a thankful guest, rise cheerfully from life's feast, and with a quiet mind go take thy rest?

LUCRETIUS

DO NOT GO GENTLE INTO THAT GOOD NIGHT

Do not go gentle into that good night,
Old age should burn and rave at close of day;
Rage, rage against the dying of the light.

Though wise men at their end know dark is right,
Because their words had forked no lightning they
Do not go gentle into that good night.

Good men, the last wave by, crying how bright
Their frail deeds might have danced in a green bay,
Rage, rage against the dying of the light.

Wild men who caught and sang the sun in flight,
And learn, too late, they grieved it on its way,
Do not go gentle into that good night.

Grave men, near death, who see with blinding sight
Blind eyes could blaze like meteors and be gay,
Rage, rage against the dying of the light.

And you, my father, there on the sad height,
Curse, bless, me now with your fierce tears, I pray.
Do not go gentle into that good night,
Rage, rage against the dying of the light.

DYLAN THOMAS

CHAPTER TWELVE

BIBLICAL SELECTIONS FOR THE SERVICE

There are many possible biblical selections for reading at a funeral or memorial service. There are themes of hope, trust in God, the expectation of a better life, forgiveness, redemption, and virtue. Many people will have their own favorites. Here are some from both the Old and the New Testaments (King James Version) that might be appropriate.

THE OLD TESTAMENT

JOB 19:21–27

21. Have pity upon me, have pity upon me, O ye my friends; for the hand of God hath touched me.
22. Why do ye persecute me as God, and are not satisfied with my flesh?
23. Oh that my words were now written! oh that they were printed in a book!
24. That they were graven with an iron pen and lead in the rock for ever!
25. For I know that my Redeemer liveth, and that he shall stand at the latter day upon the earth:

26. And though, after my skin, worms destroy this body, yet in my flesh shall I see God:

27. Whom I shall see for myself, and mine eyes shall behold, and not another; though my reins be consumed within me.

ISAIAH 25:6–9

6. And in this mountain shall the lord of hosts make unto all people a feast of fat things, a feast of wines on the lees, the lees well refined.

7. And he will destroy in this mountain the face of the covering cast over all people, and the veil that is spread over all nations.

8. He will swallow up death in victory; and the Lord God will wipe away tears from off all faces; and the rebuke of his people shall he take away from off all the earth: for the Lord hath spoken it.

9. And it shall be said in that day, Lo, this is our God; we have waited for him, and he will save us: this is the Lord; we have waited for him, we will be glad and rejoice in his salvation.

ISAIAH 61:1–3

1. The spirit of the Lord God is upon me; because the Lord hath anointed me to preach good tidings unto the meek: he hath sent me to bind up the brokenhearted, to proclaim liberty to the captives, and the opening of the prison to them that are bound;

2. To proclaim the acceptable year of the Lord, and the day of vengeance of our God; to comfort all that mourn;

3. To appoint unto them that mourn in Zion, to give unto them beauty for ashes, the oil of joy for mourning, the garment of praise for the spirit of heaviness; that they might be called trees of righteousness, the plaiting of the Lord, that he might be glorified.

LAMENTATIONS 3:22–26, 31–33

22. It is of the Lord's mercies that we are not consumed, because his compassions fail not.

23. They are new every morning: great is thy faithfulness.

24. The Lord is my portion, saith my soul; therefore will I hope in him.

25. The Lord is good unto them that wait for him, to the soul that
    seeketh him.
26. It is good that a man should both hope and quietly wait for the sal-
    vation of the Lord.

31. For the Lord will not cast off for ever:
32. But though he cause grief, yet will he have compassion according
    to the multitude of his mercies.
33. For he doth not afflict willingly, nor grieve the children of men.

THE SIXTEENTH PSALM: "IN THEE DO I PUT MY TRUST"

Preserve me, O God:
    For in thee do I put my trust.
O my soul, thou hast said unto the Lord,
    "Thou art my Lord: my goodness extendeth not to thee."
But to the saints that are in the earth,
    and to the excellent, in whom is all my delight.
Their sorrows shall be multiplied
    that hasten after another god:
    Their drink offerings of blood will I not offer,
    nor take up their names into my lips.
The Lord is the portion of mine inheritance and of my cup:
    Thou maintainest my lot.
The lines are fallen unto me in pleasant places;
    yea, I have a goodly heritage.
I will bless the Lord, who hath given me counsel;
    my reins also instruct me in the night seasons.
I have set the Lord always before me:
    Because he is at my right hand,
    I shall not be moved.
Therefore my heart is glad, and my glory rejoiceth;
    my flesh also shall rest in hope.
For thou wilt not leave my soul in hell;
    neither wilt thou suffer thine Holy One
    to see corruption.
Thou wilt show me the path of life:

In thy presence is fulness of joy;
at thy right hand there are pleasures for evermore.

THE TWENTY-THIRD PSALM

The Lord is my shepherd;
I shall not want.
He maketh me to lie down in green pastures;
he leadeth me beside the still waters.
He restoreth my soul:
he leadeth me in the paths of righteousness
for his name's sake.
Yea, though I walk through the valley
of the shadow of death,
I will fear no evil: for thou art with me;
thy rod and thy staff they comfort me.
Thou preparest a table before me
in the presence of mine enemies:
Thou anointest my head with oil;
my cup runneth over.
Surely goodness and mercy shall follow me
all the days of my life:
and I will dwell in the house of the Lord for ever.

THE TWENTY-SEVENTH PSALM

The Lord is my light and my salvation;
whom shall I fear?
the Lord is the strength of my life;
of whom shall I be afraid?
When the wicked, even mine enemies and my foes,
came upon me to eat up my flesh,
they stumbled and fell.
Though an host should encamp against me,
my heart shall not fear:
though war should rise against me,
in this will I be confident.

One thing have I desired of the Lord, that will I seek after;
    that I may dwell in the house of the Lord
    all the days of my life,
    to behold the beauty of the Lord,
    and to inquire in his temple.
For in the time of trouble he shall hide me in his pavilion:
    in the secret of his tabernacle shall he hide me;
    he shall set me up upon a rock.
And now shall mine head be lifted up above
    mine enemies round about me:
    therefore will I offer in his tabernacle sacrifices of joy;
    I will sing, yea, I will sing praises unto the Lord.
Hear, O Lord, when I cry with my voice:
    have mercy also upon me, and answer me.
When thou saidst, "Seek ye my face;"
    my heart said unto thee,
    Thy face, Lord, will I seek,
Hide not thy face far from me;
    put not thy servant away in anger:
    thou has been my help;
    leave me not, neither forsake me,
    O God of my salvation.
When my father and my mother forsake me,
    then the Lord will take me up.
Teach me thy way, O Lord,
    and lead me in a plain path,
    because of mine enemies.
Deliver me not over unto the will of mine enemies:
    for false witnesses are risen up against me,
    and such as breathe out cruelty.
I had fainted unless I had believed
    to see the goodness of the Lord
    in the land of the living.
Wait on the Lord:
    be of good courage,
    and he shall strengthen thine heart:
    wait, I say, on the Lord.

THE THIRTY-NINTH PSALM: "MY HOPE IS IN THEE"

I said, I will take heed to my ways,
     that I sin not with my tongue:
     I will keep my mouth with a bridle,
     while the wicked is before me.
I was dumb with silence, I held my peace, even from good;
     and my sorrow was stirred.
My heart was hot within me,
     while I was musing the fire burned:
     then spake I with my tongue,
Lord, make me to know mine end,
     and the measure of my days, what it is;
     that I may know how frail I am.
Behold, thou hast made my days as a handbreath;
     and mine age is as nothing before thee:
     verily every man at his best state is altogether vanity.
Surely every man walketh in a vain show;
     surely they are disquieted in vain:
     he heapeth up riches, and knoweth not
     who shall gather them.
And now, Lord, what wait I for?
     my hope is in thee.
Deliver me from all my transgressions:
     make me not the reproach of the foolish.
I was dumb, I opened not my mouth;
     because thou didst it.
Remove thy stroke away from me:
     I am consumed by the blow of thine hand.
When thou with rebukes dost correct man for iniquity,
     thou makest his beauty to consume away like a moth;
     surely every man is vanity.
Hear my prayer, O Lord, and give ear unto my cry;
     hold not thy peace at my tears:
     for I am a stranger with thee,
     and a sojourner, as all my fathers were.

O spare me, that I may recover strength,
  before I go hence, and be no more.

THE FORTY-SECOND PSALM

As the hart panteth after the water brooks,
  so panteth my soul after thee, O God.
My soul thirsteth for God, for the living God:
  when shall I come and appear before God?
My tears have been my meat day and night,
  while they continually say unto me,
  Where is thy God?
When I remember these things, I pour out my soul in me:
  for I had gone with the multitude,
  I went with them to the house of God,
  with the voice of joy and praise,
  with a multitude that kept holyday.
Why art thou cast down, O my soul?
  and why art thou disquieted in me?
  hope thou in God: for I shall yet praise him
  for the help of his countenance.
O my God, my soul is cast down within me:
  therefore will I remember thee from the land of Jordan,
  and of the Hermonites, from the hill Mizar.
Deep calleth unto deep at the noise of thy waterspouts:
  all thy waves and thy billows are gone over me.
Yet the Lord will command
  his lovingkindness in the daytime,
  and in the night his song shall be with me,
  and my prayer unto the God of my life.
I will say unto God my rock,
  Why hast thou forgotten me?
  why go I mourning
  because of the oppression of the enemy?
As with a sword in my bones,
  mine enemies reproach me,

while they say daily unto me;
    Where is thy God?
Why art thou cast down, O my soul?
    and why art thou disquieted within me?
    hope thou in God: for I shall yet praise him,
    who is the health of my countenance, and my God.

THE FORTY-SIXTH PSALM: "OUR REFUGE AND STRENGTH"

God is our refuge and strength,
    a very present help in trouble.
Therefore will not we fear,
    though the earth be removed,
    and though the mountains be carried
    into the midst of the sea;
Though the waters thereof roar
    and be troubled,
    though the mountains shake
    with the swelling thereof.
There is a river, the streams whereof
    shall make glad the city of God,
    the holy place of the tabernacles of the most High.
God is in the midst of her;
    she shall not be moved:
    God shall help her,
    and that right early.
The heathen raged,
    the kingdoms were moved.
    he uttered his voice,
    the earth melted.
The Lord of hosts is with us;
    the God of Jacob is our refuge.
Come, behold the works of the Lord,
    what desolations he hath made in the earth.
He maketh wars to cease
    unto the end of the earth;

 he breaketh the bow,
     and cutteth the spear in sunder;
     he burneth the chariot in the fire.
 Be still, and know that I am God:
     I will be exalted among the heathen,
     I will be exalted in the earth.
 The Lord of hosts is with us;
     the God of Jacob is our refuge.

THE NINETIETH PSALM:
"THOU HAST BEEN OUR DWELLING PLACE"

Lord, thou hast been our dwelling place
    in all generations.
Before the mountains were brought forth,
    or ever thou hadst formed the earth and the world,
    even from everlasting to everlasting,
    thou art God.
Thou turnest man to destruction;
    and sayest, Return, ye children of men.
For a thousand years in thy sight
    are but as yesterday when it is past,
    and as a watch in the night.
Thou carriest them away as with a flood,
    they are as a sleep:
    in the morning they are like grass which groweth up;
In the morning it flourisheth, and groweth up;
    in the evening it is cut down, and withereth.
For we are consumed by thine anger,
    and by thy wrath are we troubled.
Thou hast set our iniquities before thee,
    our secret sins in the light of thy countenance.
For all our days are passed away in thy wrath;
    we spend our years as a tale that is told.
The days of our years are threescore years and ten;
    and if by reason of strength they be fourscore years,

yet is their strength labour and sorrow;
    for it is soon cut off, and we fly away.
Who knoweth the power of thine anger?
    even according to thy fear, so is thy wrath.
So teach us to number our days,
    that we may apply our hearts unto wisdom.
Return, O Lord, how long?
    and let it repent thee concerning thy servants.
O satisfy us early with thy mercy;
    that we may rejoice and be glad all our days.
Make us glad according to the days
    wherein thou hast afflicted us,
    and the years wherein we have seen evil.
Let thy work appear unto thy servants,
    and thy glory unto their children.
And let the beauty of the Lord our God be upon us:
    and establish thou the work of our hands upon us;
    yea, the work of our hands establish thou it.

THE ONE HUNDRED SIXTEENTH PSALM

I love the Lord, because he hath heard
    my voice and my supplications.
Because he hath inclined his ear unto me,
    therefore will I call upon him as long as I live.
The sorrows of death compassed me,
    and the pains of hell gat hold upon me:
    I found trouble and sorrow.
Then called I upon the name of the Lord:
O Lord, I beseech thee, deliver my soul.
Gracious is the Lord, and righteous;
    yea, our God is merciful.
The Lord preserveth the simple:
    I was brought low, and he helped me.
Return unto thy rest, O my soul;
    for the Lord has dealt bountifully with thee.

For thou hast delivered my soul from death,
    mine eyes from tears,
    and my feet from falling.
I will walk before the Lord
    in the land of the living.
I believed, therefore have I spoken:
    I was greatly afflicted:
I said in my haste,
    All men are liars.
What shall I render unto the Lord
    for all his benefits toward me?
I will take the cup of salvation,
    and call upon the name of the Lord.
    I will pay my vows unto the Lord
    now in the presence of all his people.
Precious in the sight of the Lord
    is the death of his saints.
O Lord, truly I am thy servant;
    I am thy servant,
    and the son of thine handmaid:
    thou hast loosed my bonds.
I will offer to thee the sacrifice of thanksgiving,
    and will call upon the name of the Lord.
I will pay my vows unto the Lord
    now in the presence of all his people,
In the courts of the Lord's house,
    in the midst of thee, O Jerusalem.
    Praise ye the Lord.

THE ONE HUNDRED TWENTY-FIRST PSALM

I will lift up mine eyes unto the hills;
    from whence cometh my help.
My help cometh from the Lord,
    which made heaven and earth.
He will not suffer thy foot to be moved:

He that keepeth thee will not slumber.
Behold, he that keepeth Israel
    shall neither slumber nor sleep.
The Lord is thy keeper:
    the Lord is thy shade upon thy right hand.
The sun shall not smite thee by day,
    nor the moon by night.
The Lord shall preserve thee from all evil:
    he shall preserve thy soul.
The Lord shall preserve thy going out and thy coming in
    from this time forth, and even for evermore.

THE ONE HUNDRED THIRTIETH PSALM

Out of the depths have I cried unto thee, O Lord.
Lord, hear my voice:
  let thine ears be attentive to the voice of my supplications.
If thou, Lord, shouldest mark iniquities,
    O Lord, who shall stand?
But there is forgiveness with thee,
    that thou mayest be feared.
I wait for the Lord, my soul doth wait,
    and in his word do I hope.
My soul waiteth for the Lord
    more than they that watch for the morning:
    I say, more than they that watch for the morning.
Let Israel hope in the Lord:
    for with the Lord there is mercy,
    and with him is plenteous redemption.
And he shall redeem Israel from all his iniquities.

THE ONE HUNDRED THIRTY-NINTH PSALM, 1–17

O Lord, thou hast searched me, and known me.
Thou knowest my downsitting and mine uprising,
    thou understandeth my thought afar off.

Thou compassest my path and my lying down,
   and art acquainted with all my ways.
For there is not a word in my tongue,
   but lo, O Lord, thou knowest it altogether.
Thou hast beset me behind and before,
   and laid thine hand upon me.
Such knowledge is too wonderful for me;
   it is high, I cannot attain unto it.
Whither shall I go from thy spirit.
   or whither shall I flee from thy presence?
If I ascend up into heaven, thou art there:
   If I make my bed in hell, behold, thou art there.
If I take the wings of the morning,
   and dwell in the uttermost parts of the sea;
Even there shall thy hand lead me,
   and thy right hand shall hold me.
If I say, Surely the darkness shall cover me,
   even the night shall be light about me;
Yea, the darkness hideth not from thee;
   but the night shineth as the day:
   the darkness and light are both alike to thee.
For thou hast possessed my reins:
   thou hast covered me in my mother's womb.
I will praise thee; for I am fearfully and wonderfully made:
   marvellous are thy works;
   and that my soul knoweth right well.
My substance was not hid from thee,
   when I was made in secret,
   and curiously wrought
   in the lowest parts of the earth.
Thine eyes did see my substance, yet being unperfect;
   and in thy book all my members were written,
   which in continuance were fashioned,
   when as yet there was none of them.
How precious also are thy thoughts unto me, O God!
   how great is the sum of them!

ECCLESIASTES

To everything there is a season,
  and a time to every purpose under the heaven.
A time to be born, and a time to die;
  a time to plant, and a time to pluck up that which is planted;
A time to kill, and a time to heal;
  a time to break down, and a time to build up;
A time to weep, and a time to laugh;
  a time to mourn, and a time to dance;
A time to cast away stones, and a time to gather stones together;
  a time to embrace, and a time to refrain from embracing;
A time to seek, and a time to lose;
  a time to keep, and a time to cast away;
A time to rend, and a time to sew;
  a time to keep silence, and a time to speak;
A time to love, and a time to hate;
  a time for war, and a time for peace.

THE NEW TESTAMENT

1 JOHN 3:1–2

1. Behold, what manner of love the Father hath bestowed upon us, that we should be called the sons of God: therefore the world knoweth us not, because it knew him not.

2. Beloved, now are we the sons of God; and it doth not yet appear what we shall be: but we know that, when he shall appear, we shall be like him; for we shall see him as he is.

JOHN 5:24–27

24. Verily, verily, I say unto you, He that heareth my word, and believeth on him that sent me, hath everlasting life, and shall not come into condemnation; but is passed from death unto life.

25. Verily, verily, I say unto you, The hour is coming, and now is, when the dead shall hear the voice of the Son of God: and they that hear shall live.
26. For as the Father hath life in himself; so hath he given to the Son to have life in himself;
27. And hath given him authority to execute judgment also, because he is the Son of man.

JOHN 6:37–40

37. All that the Father giveth me shall come to me; and him that cometh to me I will in no wise cast out.
38. For I came down from heaven, not to do mine own will, but the will of him that sent me.
39. And this is the Father's will which hath sent me, that of all which he hath given me I should lose nothing, but should raise it up again at the last day.
40. And this is the will of him that sent me, that every one which seeth the Son, and believeth on him, may have everlasting life: and I will raise him up at the last day.

JOHN 10:11–16

11. I am the good shepherd: the good shepherd giveth his life for the sheep.
12. But he that is an hireling, and not the shepherd, whose own the sheep are not, seeth the wolf coming, and leaveth the sheep, and fleeth: and the wolf catcheth them, and scattereth the sheep.
13. The hireling fleeth, because he is an hireling, and careth not for the sheep.
14. I am the good shepherd, and know my sheep, and am known of mine.
15. As the Father knoweth me, even so know I the Father: and I lay down my life for the sheep.
16. And other sheep I have, which are not of this fold: them also I must bring, and they shall hear my voice; and there shall be one fold, and one shepherd.

JOHN 11:21–27

21. Then said Martha unto Jesus, Lord, if thou hadst been here, my brother had not died.
22. But I know, that even now, whatsoever thou wilt ask of God, God will give it thee.
23. Jesus saith unto her, Thy brother shall rise again.
24. Martha saith unto him, I know that he shall rise again in the resurrection at the last day.
25. Jesus said unto her, I am the resurrection, and the life: he that believeth in me, though he were dead, yet shall he live:
26. And whosoever liveth and believeth in me shall never die. Believest thou this?
27. She saith unto him, Yea, Lord; I believe that thou art the Christ, the Son of God, which should come into the world.

JOHN 14:1–6

1. Let not your heart be troubled: ye believe in God, believe also in me.
2. In my Father's house are many mansions: if it were not so, I would have told you. I go to prepare a place for you.
3. And if I go and prepare a place for you, I will come again, and receive you unto myself; that where I am, there ye may be also.
4. And whither I go ye know, and the way ye know.
5. Thomas saith unto him, Lord, we know not whither thou goest; and how can we know the way?
6. Jesus saith unto him, I am the way, and the truth, and the life: no man cometh unto the Father, but by me.

ROMANS 6:3–5

3. Know ye not, that so many of us as were baptized into Jesus Christ were baptized into his death?
4. Therefore we are buried with him by baptism into death; that like as Christ was raised up from the dead by the glory of the Father, even so we also should walk in newness of life.

5. For if we have been planted together in the likeness of his death, we shall be also in the likeness of his resurrection:

ROMANS 8:14–19, 34–35, 37–39

14. For as many as are led by the Spirit of God, they are the sons of God.
15. For ye have not received the spirit of bondage again to fear; but ye have received the Spirit of adoption, whereby we cry, Abba, Father.
16. The Spirit itself beareth witness with our spirit, that we are the children of God:
17. And if children, then heirs; heirs of God, and joint-heirs with Christ; if so be that we suffer with him, that we may be also glorified together.
18. For I reckon that the sufferings of this present time are not worthy to be compared with the glory which shall be revealed in us.
19. For the earnest expectation of the creature waiteth for the manifestation of the sons of God.

34. Who is he that condemneth? It is Christ that died, yea rather, that is risen again, who is even at the right hand of God, who also maketh intercession for us.
35. Who shall separate us from the love of Christ? shall tribulation, or distress, or persecution, or famine, or nakedness, or peril, or sword?

37. Nay, in all these things we are more than conquerors, through him that loved us.
38. For I am persuaded that neither death, nor life, nor angels, nor principalities, nor powers, nor things present, nor things to come,
39. Nor height, nor depth, nor any other creature, shall be able to separate us from the love of God, which is in Christ Jesus our Lord.

1 CORINTHIANS 15:20–26, 35–38, 42–44, 53–58

20. But now is Christ risen from the dead, and become the first fruits of them that slept.

21. For since by man came death, by man came also the resurrection of the dead.
22. For as in Adam all die, even so in Christ shall all be made alive.
23. But every man in his own order; Christ the first fruits; afterward they that are Christ's, at his coming.
24. Then cometh the end, when he shall have delivered up the kingdom to God, even the Father; when he shall have put down all rule and all authority and power.
25. For he must reign, till he hath put all enemies under his feet.
26. The last enemy that shall be destroyed is death.

35. But some man will say, How are the dead raised up? and with what body do they come?
36. Thou fool! that which thou sowest is not quickened, except it die:
37. And that which thou sowest, thou sowest not that body that shall be, but bare grain, it may chance of wheat, or of some other grain:
38. But God giveth it a body as it hath pleased him, and to every seed his own body.

42. So also is the resurrection of the dead. It is sown in corruption; it is raised in incorruption:
43. It is sown in dishonour; it is raised in glory: it is sown in weakness; it is raised in power.
44. It is sown a natural body; it is raised a spiritual body. There is a natural body, and there is a spiritual body.

53. For this corruptible must put on incorruption, and this mortal must put on immortality.
54. So when this corruptible shall have put on incorruption, and this mortal shall have put on immortality, then shall be brought to pass the saying that is written, Death is swallowed up in victory.
55. O death, where is thy sting? O grave, where is thy victory?
56. The sting of death is sin; and the strength of sin is the law.
57. But thanks be to God, which giveth us the victory through our Lord Jesus Christ.
58. Therefore, my beloved brethren, be ye steadfast, unmovable, always abounding in the work of the Lord, forasmuch as ye know that your labor is not in vain in the Lord.

2 CORINTHIANS 4:16–18, 5:1–5

16. For which cause we faint not; but though our outward man perish, yet the inward man is renewed day by day.

17. For our light affliction, which is but for a moment, worketh for us a far more exceeding and eternal weight of glory;

18. While we look not at the things which are seen, but at the things which are not seen: for the things which are seen are temporal; but the things which are not seen are eternal.

1. For we know that if our earthly house of this tabernacle were dissolved, we have a building of God, an house not made with hands, eternal in the heavens.

2. For in this we groan, earnestly desiring to be clothed upon with our house which is from heaven:

3. If so be that being clothed we shall not be found naked.

4. For we that are in this tabernacle do groan, being burdened: not for that we would be unclothed, but clothed upon, that mortality might be swallowed up of life.

5. Now he that hath wrought us for the selfsame thing is God, who also hath given unto us the earnest of the Spirit.

1 THESSALONIANS 4:13–18

13. But I would not have you to be ignorant, brethren, concerning them which are asleep, that ye sorrow not, even as others which have no hope.

14. For if we believe that Jesus died and rose again, even so them also which sleep in Jesus will God bring with him.

15. For this we say unto you by the word of the Lord, that we which are alive, and remain unto the coming of the Lord, shall not prevent them which are asleep.

16. For the Lord himself shall descend from heaven with a shout, with the voice of the archangel, and with the trump of God: and the dead in Christ shall rise first:

17. Then we which are alive and remain shall be caught up together with them in the clouds, to meet the Lord in the air: and so shall we ever be with the Lord.

18. Wherefore comfort one another with these words.

REVELATION 7:9–17

9. After this I beheld, and, lo, a great multitude, which no man could number, of all nations, and kindreds, and people, and tongues, stood before the throne, and before the Lamb, clothed with white robes, and palms in their hands;

10. And cried with a loud voice, saying, Salvation to our God which sitteth upon the throne, and unto the Lamb.

11. And all the angels stood round about the throne, and about the elders and the four beasts, and fell before the throne on their faces, and worshipped god.

12. Saying, Amen: Blessing, and glory, and wisdom, and thanksgiving, and honour, and power, and might be unto our God for ever and ever. Amen.

13. And one of the elders answered, saying unto me, What are these which are arrayed in white robes? and whence came they?

14. And I said unto him, Sir, thou knowest. And he said to me, These are they which came out of great tribulation, and have washed their robes, and made them white in the blood of the Lamb.

15. Therefore are they before the throne of God, and serve him day and night in his temple: and he that sitteth on the throne shall dwell among them.

16. They shall hunger no more, neither thirst any more; neither shall the sun light on them, nor any heat.

17. For the Lamb, which is in the midst of the throne, shall feed them, and shall lead them unto living fountains of waters: and God shall wipe away all tears from their eyes.

REVELATION 21:2–7

2. And I John saw the holy city, new Jerusalem, coming down from God out of heaven, prepared as a bride adorned for her husband.

3. And I heard a great voice out of heaven, saying, Behold, the tabernacle of God is with men, and he will dwell with them, and they shall be his people, and God himself shall be with them, and be their God.

4. And God shall wipe away all tears from their eyes; and there shall be no more death, neither sorrow, nor crying, neither shall there be any more pain: for the former things are passed away.

5. And he that sat upon the throne said, Behold, I make all things new. And he said unto me, Write: for these words are true and faithful.

6. And he said unto me, It is done. I am Alpha and Omega, the beginning and the end. I will give unto him that is athirst of the fountain of the water of life freely.

7. He that overcometh shall inherit all things; and I will be his God, and he shall be my son.

CHAPTER THIRTEEN

MUSIC FOR THE SERVICE

The following suggestions can be used as a reference for those who plan to use musical offerings in a memorial service. If you intend to hire a vocalist, pianist, organist, or instrumental group, you can give them specific requests for songs. Alternatively, you can use audiotapes or compact discs at the service.

Close friends and family will likely recall what type of music the deceased most preferred. Go through his own music collection to get ideas. If the deceased had church affiliations, religious or gospel music may be appropriate. There is also a large body of classical music in a sacred tradition that could be appropriate. Moreover, much of blues, jazz, folk, rock, and country music also has religious themes.

One advantage of using recordings is that you can choose the exact mood you want. Many songs have been recorded in different styles and by artists with very different traditions. "Amazing Grace," for example, can be found in almost every style, from near-operatic to bagpipe. In the list that follows, a selection of recording artists is included. In the case of classical music, the album number is included.

CLASSICAL

Traditionally, memorial services used somber musical pieces in a minor mode. Now families often choose several pieces which are more uplifting and which emphasize redemption.

"Agnus Dei," the famous text from the Catholic liturgy, is the vocal setting of Samuel Barber's "Adagio for Strings," performed by the Robert Shaw Festival Strings. It is on the CD titled *Evocation of the Spirit* (Telarc 80406-2).

"Choral Evensong for Ascension Day" has been recorded by the King's College Choir (EMI 65102-2).

"Jesu, Joy of Man's Desiring" by Johann Sebastian Bach, Cantata 147, has been recorded by John Eliot Gardiner and the Monteverdi Choir, English Baroque Soloists (Archiv 439885-2).

"I Know My Redeemer Liveth" from Handel's *Messiah* was recorded by Robert Shaw and the Atlanta Symphony Orchestra and Chorus (Telarc 80093-2).

"Pie Jesu." Part of the requiem mass was used by the French composer Gabriel Fauré in his "Requiem." An excellent version was recorded by Robert Shaw and the Atlanta Symphony and Chorus (Telarc 80135-2).

"Requiem" by Wolfgang Amadeus Mozart. Recorded by John Eliot Gardiner and the Monteverdi Choir, English Baroque Soloists (Philips 420-197-2).

Johann Sebastian Bach's organ pieces are often used at funerals and memorial services, even though many are in a major key. Some have been recorded by the organist E. Power Biggs; see *Bach: Great Organ Favorites* (CBS 42644-2).

The Lord's Prayer in the version by Albert Hay Malotte can be found on the cassette "Lord's Prayer"/"How Great Thou Art," sung by Jim Nabors (CBS 40450-4).

The Twenty-third Psalm has been used by the English composer John Rutter as part of his "Requiem"; see John Rutter and the Cambridge Singers (Collegium Records 103-2).

"When I'm Laid in Earth" is an aria from the first English-language opera, *Dido and Aeneas,* by Henry Purcell. Jessye Norman sings Dido's lament on Phillips 416299-2.

St. *Matthew Passion* by J. S. Bach was recorded by John Eliot Gardiner and the Monteverdi Choir (Archiv 427648-2).

Schubert Masses 2 and 6 have been recorded by Robert Shaw and the Atlanta Symphony Orchestra and Chorus (Telarc 80212-2). Schubert masses are in a major key but are still appropriate.

Beethoven Symphony No. 7, Movement 2. The second movement of Beethoven's Seventh Symphony, the "Funeral March," is rather like a processional march and is frequently used in funerals. Numerous versions of it are available, usually combining the Seventh with a recording of another Beethoven symphony on the same CD. It has been done by the Berlin, Chicago, Columbia, Cleveland, London, and BBC orchestras.

Beethoven String Quartets are played by the Tokyo String Quartet (RCA 61621-2).

Brahms Quintets played by the Cleveland String Quartet are on Telmarc 80346-2.

In Jewish temples traditional, somber pieces are often used. Some have been recorded by the operatic tenor Richard Tucker on the title **Kol Nidre Service** (Sony 35207-2).

TRADITIONAL FOLK SONGS

"Amazing Grace" is by far the most frequently played folk hymn at funerals and memorial services. It has been played in all styles of music and on all instruments from bagpipes to symphony orchestras. For instrumentals, there are versions by the Boston Pops, Canadian Brass, 101 Strings, and Zamfir. Judy Collins has recorded a stirring contemporary version. For country, try Willie Nelson or the Nitty Gritty Dirt Band.

"Flowers of the Forest" is a traditional dirge. It has been recorded by the Levellers, Open House, June Tabor, and Irene Worth.

"Greensleeves." This lovely and melancholy tune has been recorded by Chet Atkins, John Coltrane, Paul Desmond and the Modern Jazz Quartet, James Galway, Modern Jazz Quartet, Wes Montgomery, Olivia Newton-John, Oscar Peterson, Shorty Rogers, John Rutter and the Cambridge Singers, Pete Seeger, Kiri Te Kanawa, the Weavers, and Roger Whittaker.

"Scotland the Brave." This dirge is a favorite of bagpipers. See recordings by Louis Clark and the Royal Philharmonic, Bill Clement, Original Cast—Forever Plaid, Gary Glitter, Gordon Highlanders, Royal Scots Dragoon Guards, Tommy Scott Pipes and Dixie Band, and Scottish National Pipe and Drum.

"Simple Gifts." This folk classic has been recorded by many performing artists and appears in other works as well. Aaron Copland used this melody as a theme in his Appalachian Spring. See works by Judy Collins, William Coulter/Barry Phillips, the Mormon Tabernacle Choir, Raffi, Harvey Reid, Kevin Roth, and Shinobu Sato.

ROCK/POP

"All My Friends." Gregg Allman and Cowboy.

"Bridge over Troubled Water." The original and most famous version was recorded by Simon and Garfunkel. You can also find versions by Roberta Flack, Aretha Franklin, the Mormon Tabernacle Choir, and the Boston Pops.

"Crying in the Chapel" was recorded in a popular version by Elvis Presley.

"**Everything Happens for a Reason.**" The Floaters.

"**Funeral for a Friend.**" Elton John.

"**Goodbye My Friend.**" Karla Bonoff, Linda Ronstadt.

"**Go Rest High on the Mountain.**" Vince Gill.

"**I'll Go to My Grave Loving You.**" Statler Brothers.

"**I'll Remember You.**" Bob Dylan.

"**In This Life.**" Madonna, Gladys Knight, Bette Midler, Collin Raye, Kirk Whalum.

"**Knocking on Heaven's Door**" is associated with Eric Clapton, Randy Crawford, and Guns 'n Roses. Also see the 30th Anniversary All Star Band, Bob Dylan, Jerry Garcia, the Heart of Gold Band, and Arthur Lewis.

"**The Last Song.**" Elton John.

"**Last Train Home.**" Armoured Saint.

"**Life Is Too Short.**" Too $hort.

"**A Little Fall of Rain.**" From the musical *Les Misérables*.

"**The Long and Winding Road**" was written by John Lennon and Paul McCartney and recorded by the Beatles. It has also been recorded by Aretha Franklin, Olivia Newton-John, and Wings.

"**Many Rivers to Cross.**" A reggae classic as recorded by Jimmy Cliff. Also recorded by Oleta Adams, Joe Cocker, Harry Nilsson, Linda Ronstadt, Stanley Turrentine, and UB-40.

"**Morning Has Broken**" is best known in the version by Cat Stevens.

It has also been recorded by Neil Diamond, Sally Harmon, John MacNally, Nana Mouskouri, Songs of the Highlands, and Roger Whittaker.

"Mr. Tambourine Man" was a Bob Dylan hit. The Barbarians, The Byrds, Roger McGuinn, Melanie, William Shatner, Frankie Valli, and Stevie Wonder have also recorded it.'

"November Rain." Guns 'n Roses.

"Sometimes I Feel like a Motherless Child." This is a haunting traditional black American spiritual. Look for versions by Louis Armstrong, Marilyn Horne, Odetta, and Paul Robeson.

"Song for Adam." Jackson Browne.

"Stairway to Heaven." Led Zeppelin.

"Sunshine on My Shoulder." Sung by John Denver. See also Floyd Cramer, 101 Strings, and Billy Vaughn.

"Tears in Heaven" was written and recorded by Eric Clapton to memorialize the death of his infant son.

"Turn! Turn! Turn!" The musical adaptation of Ecclesiastes' "To everything there is a season," first recorded by the Byrds. Also recorded by Pete Seeger and Judy Collins.

"Will the Circle Be Unbroken?" The Nitty Gritty Dirt Band is associated with this song. It has also been recorded by Blind James Campbell, "Ramblin'" Jack Elliot, Arlo Guthrie, Jerry Lee Lewis, and Willie Nelson.

"Yesterday." This Beatles classic has been recorded by dozens of artists in a wide variety of styles, from classical to country. You can find versions by Placido Domingo, Marvin Gaye, Benny Goodman, Merle Haggard,

The King's Singers, André Kostelanetz, the London Symphony Orchestra, Elvis Presley, Frank Sinatra, Roger Williams, and Zamfir.

"You've Got a Friend." James Taylor. Also recorded by Count Basie, Jimmy Dorsey, Ella Fitzgerald, Roberta Flack, Donny Hathaway, Michael Jackson, Carole King, The Persuasions, Barbra Streisand, and BeBe Winans.

MUSICALS AND STANDARDS

"Climb Every Mountain." From *The Sound of Music.* Pop versions have been recorded by Tony Bennett, the Four Tops, Mary Martin, the Mormon Tabernacle Choir, Kate Smith, and Kiri Te Kanawa.

"Dream a Little Dream of Me." Mama Cass's theme song. There are also versions by Louis Armstrong, Chicago, Ella Fitzgerald, Henry Mancini, Dean Martin, and Ozzie Nelson.

"Harbour Lights." Rosemary Clooney, Bing Crosby, Duke Kamoku, Sammy Kaye, Wayne King, Jerry Lee Lewis, Guy Lombardo, Willie Nelson, the Platters, Elvis Presley, Billy Vaughn, Dinah Washington, Roger Whittaker.

"The Impossible Dream." From *Man of La Mancha.*

"Red Sails in the Sunset." Gene Ammons, Don Cherry, Nat "King" Cole, Bing Crosby, Fats Domino, Gracie Fields, Erroll Garner, the Platters, "Big" Joe Turner, Billy Vaughn, Slim Whitman, Roger Whittaker.

"Somewhere (There's a Place for Us)." From *West Side Story.*

"Sunrise, Sunset." From *Fiddler on the Roof.* Often used at weddings, but also appropriate for memorial services. Also recorded by Perry Como, the Mormon Tabernacle Choir, Jim Nabors, 101 Strings, and Roger Whittaker.

"You'll Never Walk Alone." From *Carousel.* Placido Domingo, Eileen Farrell, Aretha Franklin, Judy Garland, Lee Greenwood, the Mormon Tabernacle Choir, Jim Nabors, Olivia Newton-John, Elvis Presley, Royal Philharmonic Orchestra, Frank Sinatra, Kiri Te Kanawa, and Roger Williams have all recorded versions.

NEW AGE

Paul Sauvanet, *Tristesse: Five Adagios for Times of Sorrow* (HS 11057-2).

SOUL/RHYTHM AND BLUES

"Going Home." Norman Blake, Jethro Burns, Sam Bush, Vassar Clements, David Holland, Butch Robbins, Tut Taylor, Johnathan Butler, Rod Erickson, Kenny G, Red Garland, Al Jones, Sam McNeil, Art Pepper, Elvis Presley, Pure Prairie League, Paul Robeson, Santana, Ron Shaw, Muddy Waters.

"Light of Day" was recorded by the Lumzy Sisters on their Atlantic CD *Memories.*

"Precious Lord." Clarence Fountain, Little Richard, Beau Williams.

"Soon I Will Be Done with the Troubles of This World," a traditional melody, has been recorded by Carla Bley and Steve Swallow.

JAZZ/BIG BAND/BEBOP

While Duke Ellington did compose some sacred music, little jazz has been written specifically for funerals. Nonetheless, jazz selections remain popular because of their melancholy themes of loss.

"Caravan" is an old Duke Ellington tune. Dizzy Gillespie also made a famous recording. Other artists who have recorded it include Chet

Atkins, Art Blakey, Bob Brookmeyer, Dave Brubeck, Charlie Byrd, Vassar Clements, Nat "King" Cole, Eddie Condon, Harry Connick, Jr., and Bobby Darin.

"Come Sunday" was also written by Duke Ellington. It has been performed by Cannonball Adderly, Louis Bellson, Dave Burrell, Duke Ellington, Earl "Fatha" Hines, Johnny Hodges, Dick Hyman, Milt Jackson, Frankie Laine, Yusef Lateef, Ramsey Lewis, MJQ, the New York Trumpet Ensemble, Oscar Peterson, André Previn, Clark Terry, Ben Webster, and Joe Williams.

"Don't Get Around Much Any More" is another Ellington number. It has been recorded by Louis Armstrong, Louis Bellson, Tony Bennett, Dave Brubeck, June Christy, Nat "King" Cole, Harry Connick, Jr., Sam Cooke, Bing Crosby, Bobby Darin, Sammy Davis, Jr., Billy Eckstein, Duke Ellington, Benny Goodman, Stéphane Grappelli, Lionel Hampton, Coleman Hawkins, Earl "Fatha" Hines, the Ink Spots, Milt Jackson, Harry James, B. B. King, Paul McCartney, Willie Nelson, Oscar Peterson, John Pizzarelli, George Shearing, Mel Tormé, Ben Webster, and Teddy Wilson.

"God Bless the Child" is associated with Billie Holiday. It has also been recorded by Harry Belafonte, Tony Bennett, Blood, Sweat and Tears, Kenny Burrell, Rosemary Clooney, Art Farmer, Ella Fitzgerald, Aretha Franklin, Stéphane Grappelli, Lionel Hampton, Freddie Hubbard, Marian McPartland, Carmen MacRae, Wes Montgomery, Lou Rawls, Sonny Rollins, Diana Ross, Barbra Streisand, Cal Tjader, and Stanley Turrentine.

"I'll Be Seeing You." Ray Anthony, Tony Bennett, James Booker, Rosemary Clooney, Bing Crosby, Vic Damone, Tommy Dorsey, Lionel Hampton, Billie Holiday, Liberace, Bud Shank, George Shearing, Dinah Shore, Frank Sinatra, the Skyliners, Jo Stafford, Sarah Vaughan, Paul Weston, Roger Whittaker.

"My Way." The most popular version of this song was recorded by Frank Sinatra. It has also been sung by Brook Benton, Glen Campbell,

Richard Clayderman, Gary Oldman, Elvis Presley, Jimmy Roselli, Sex Pistols, and Nina Simone.

"When the Saints Go Marching In" has been played by nearly everyone. In New Orleans, Dixieland bands traditionally play this song to accompany the casket to the cemetery. It has been recorded by, among others, Louis Armstrong, Chris Barber's Jazz Band, Sidney Bechet, Harry Belafonte, Calimbo Steel Band, Papa Celestin, Jack Daniels Original Silver Cornet Band, "Wild" Bill Davison, Bo Diddley, Fats Domino, Dukes of Dixieland, Pete Fountain, Earl "Fatha" Hines, Al Hirt, Mahalia Jackson, Bunk Johnson, the Kingston Trio, the Mormon Tabernacle Choir, Preservation Hall Jazz Band, and Zydeco Force.

RELIGIOUS HYMNS

Religious hymns come from a variety of sources, including Martin Luther and traditional folk songs. Jazz, soul, rock, country, and classics have all made their contribution to sacred music. You may wish to pick hymns that are popular in your denomination and use local singers for the ceremony.

"Abide with Me." Gene Ammons, Dame Clara Butt, Walter Davis, Jr., Rev. Clay Evans, Ella Fitzgerald, Ruth Naomi Floyd, Tennessee Ernie Ford, Charlie Haden and Hank Jones, the Hymnworks, the Choir of Kings College, Mahalia Jackson, Pete Krebs, James Last, Mary Louis Academy, Thelonious Monk, the Mormon Tabernacle Choir, Mountain Gospel Music, Jim Nabors, John Renbourn, Richard Stoltzman, Jo Stafford and Gordon MacRae, Norma Zimmer, Jim Roberts.

"Beautiful Savior." Steve Green.

"Because He Lives." Nathan DiGesare, Garry Jones, Nelson Ned.

"Come Ye Disconsolate." Roberta Flack and Donny Hathaway, Mary Johnson Davis.

"Flowers of the Forest." The Levellers, Open House, June Tabor, Irene Worth.

"How Great Thou Art." Monty Alexander, Hamilton Clayton Jazz Orchestra, Myron Floren, Guy and Ralna, 101 Strings, Dolly Parton, Elvis Presley, Bob Ralston, Kate Smith, the Statler Brothers, Larry Stephenson.

"I Am the Bread of Life." John Michael Talbot.

"Joyful, Joyful, We Adore Thee." Crystal Lewis, Choir of Saint Mark's Church, Glad, Steve Green, Hosanna! Music, Karyn Henley and Randall Dennis, the Kingdom Song, Saint Francis Choir, CeCe Winans.

"Just a Closer Walk with Thee." Wallace Davenport, Dukes of Dixieland, Pete Fountain, Peggy Gilbert, Earl "Fatha" Hines, Thomas Jefferson/Paul Barbarin/Louis Cottrell, George Lewis New Orleans Rhythm Boys, Turk Murphy, Kid Ory, Paddock Jazz Band, Bob Scobey's Frisco Band, the Sensational Nightingales, Martin Simpson, Sarah Vaughan, Buck White.

"A Mighty Fortress Is Our God." The American Boys Choir, Tennessee Ernie Ford, Edward Gerhard, Glad, Amy Grant, Steve Green, Larnelle Harris, Mahalia Jackson, the Mormon Tabernacle Choir.

"Nearer My God to Thee." The Canadian Brass, Mississippi John Hurt, the Persuasions.

"O God Our Help in Ages Past" is popular among Episcopalians. It appears in many hymn collections, for instance in recordings by the Mormon Tabernacle Choir. Tennesee Ernie Ford also recorded it.

"Old Rugged Cross." Tom Adams, Byron Berline/John Hickman, Eddie Davis and the New York Jazz Ensemble, Herb Ellis, Mark Isham, Lonnie Johnson, George Lewis, the Mississippi Mass Choir, James Morrison, J. D. Sumner.

"O Love That Wilt Not Let Me Go." George Beverly Shea.

"On Eagle's Wings." R. Carlos Nakai, *Oklahoma City Relief Album; A Time of Healing.*

"Peace in the Valley." Margaret Allison and the Angelic Gospel Singers, John Anderson, Mike Bloomfield.

"Shall We Gather by the River" in Aaron Copland's version is on the CD *Long Time Ago,* Aaron Copland songs sung by Dawn Upshaw and Thomas Hampson.

"The Strife Is O'er, the Battle Done." God's Almighty Son.

GOSPEL MUSIC

The following suggestions are arranged by performing artist or performing group. Gospel is a specialty area of music that is almost exclusively African-American. The artists listed below perform principally in this idiom.

The top gospel recording artist is the late Reverend James Cleveland, who is regarded as the father of gospel music. Other prominent singers are Mahalia Jackson and the Mississippi Mass Choir. Numerous songs are associated with the Pentecostal Church, and gospel songs in that tradition are of concert quality. This music is almost all uplifting and not mournful.

Vanessa Belle Armstrong: *Something on the Inside, The Secret Is Out.*

Helen Baylor: *Highly Recommended, Look a Little Closer, Start All Over.*

Shirley Cesar: *Celebration, Don't Drive Your Momma Away, Faded Rose, Go, He's Working It Out for You, Her Very Best, I Remember Mama, Jesus I Love Calling Your Name, Live in Chicago, Rejoice, Sailin', Shirley Cesar Live. . . , He Will Come, Stand Still.*

Dr. Mattie Moss Clark: *Reunion of the Southwest Michigan State Choir, The National C.O.G.I.C. Music Convention Choir, The Southern California Holy Gospel Feast.*

Rev. James Cleveland: *Get Right Church, Jesus Is the Best Thing, Rev. James Cleveland & The Los Angeles Gospel Messengers, Peace Be Still.*

The Five Blind Boys: *The Best of Five Blind Boys, In the Hands of the Lord, Soon I'll Be Done, Will Jesus Be Waiting.*

Rev. Edwin Hawkins: *All Things Are Possible, Kings and Kingdoms, Rev. Edwin Hawkins Singers—Oh Happy Day.*

Tramaine Hawkins: *All My Best to You, Determined, To a Higher Place, Tramaine/Songs of Walter, Treasury.*

Cissy Houston: *Face to Face, I'll Take Care of You.*

Mahalia Jackson: *"Amazing Grace, Bless This House, Go Tell It on the Mountain, Gospels, Spirituals, and Hymns, I Sing Because I'm Happy, I'm Going to Tell God, Live at Newport 1958, Mahalia Jackson Sings America's Favorite Hymns, Mahalia Jackson Sings Best-loved Hymns of Dr. Martin Luther King, The World's Greatest Gospel Singer.*

The Jackson Southernaires: *Greatest Hits, Lord, You've Been Good to Me, O Lord I'm Still Waiting, Presenting Joy, Peace, Happiness and Love, The Word in Song.*

Rev. John P. Kee: *Colorblind, Just Me This Time, There Is Hope, Wash Me, We Walk By Faith, Yes Lord.*

Bobbie Mason: *Heritage of Faith, Standing in the Gap.*

The Mississippi Mass Choir: *God Gets the Glory, Greatest Hits, I Wanna Be Right, It Remains to Be Seen.*

New Jersey Mass Choir: *At Their Best, Heroes, Hold Up the Light, Look Up and Live.*

New Life Community Choir: *Show Up, Wait on Him.*

Dorothy Norwood: *A Mother's Son, A Wonderful Day, Golden Classics, Live, Live with the Georgia Mass Choir, Platinum Gospel, Shake the Devil Off.*

Richard Smallwood: *Adoration, Live, Portrait, Testimony.*

The Staple Singers: *Be What You Are, Beatitude: Respect Yourself, Best of the Staple Singers, Chronicle, City in the Sky, Freedom Highway, Great Day, Greatest Hits, Soul Folk in Action, The Staple Swingers, Turning Point, We'll Get Over.*

Hezekiah Walker: *Live in Atlanta at Morehouse College, Live in New York, Live in Toronto.*

Thomas Whitfield: *Alive and Satisfied.*

BASIC FUNERAL PLANNING

The death of a loved one will thrust a series of decisions upon you. In most cases, they are decisions you will be very ill prepared to make in an arena in which you have little or no experience. You will need to select a funeral home, transport a body, and find a cemetery plot. What kind of casket should you buy? What kind of gravestone is appropriate? These are extremely difficult decisions because they carry so much emotional freight with them. You may think it necessary to express your grief by buying an expensive casket, especially if there will be a viewing and other people will be aware of your choices. You may be having trouble accepting the death of someone you love and thus may be swayed by the thought of an airtight seal on the grave liner, perhaps subconsciously feeling that you may be able to retain something of the deceased longer. You may choose a large, elaborate marble marker when a small brass plate would do.

During the time immediately following a loss, it may be difficult to be a hardheaded negotiator. Nonetheless, the fact is that once the basic choice of how to handle the body after death has been made, everything else is a consumer decision. In some cases, what you may be buying is convenience—the convenience of not having to think too much about details at a time of great emotional stress. In other cases, you may be buying prestige, appearances, or the lessening of some guilt. All that is fine. During life many things—from expensive cars to big houses—are bought for those reasons.

But if you are simply buying products and services that will enable you to dispose of your loved one's body in a dignified, meaningful way, the decisions may be much easier to make, even among the many choices that will be presented to you. For example, the process of disposing of the body can be very elaborate and expensive. You can choose the full services of a funeral home, which will prepare the body for viewing and burial. It can also handle, for a price, every detail of the funeral, right down to printing acknowledgment cards. You can buy a top-of-the-line casket and grave liner, pick a riverview grave site in a beautiful cemetery, and erect an impressive marker. On the other hand, the process can be very simple: cremation in a cardboard container with the ashes returned to you to dispose of as you wish. Your range of choices is wide, so make sure you select what you really want, can afford, and believe to be most appropriate to the circumstances.

WHAT DO YOU WANT DONE WITH THE BODY?

Your first decision will govern many of your decisions. Your basic choices are burial, cremation, and donation.

BURIAL

The vast majority of Americans are still buried in the earth after death. Many religions, indeed, discourage cremation. If you choose burial, you will need to make three further selections: of a casket, a cemetery plot, and a marker. Burial is more expensive than cremation for three reasons: the cost of the plot is more expensive than the cost of a plot or a niche for cremated remains; there is more labor involved in the opening and closing of a grave; and a more substantial container is usually used for burial than for cremation.

CREMATION

In cremation the body is subjected to heat of approximately 2,200 degrees Fahrenheit for several hours, which reduces it to a coarse powder commonly referred to as ashes. They are, in fact, noncombustible bone fragments. These fragments are then returned to you in a cardboard container, and you may scatter them, keep them at home, bury them, or purchase a niche for storage. If they are kept or buried, you may wish to purchase a more substantial container.

DONATION

Some people wish to donate their remains for medical research. Arrangements for this must be made with a local medical school or other research facility. These days there is a particular interest in Alzheimer's disease research. Not all bodies, however, can be accepted. Most schools reject, for example, bodies that have been seriously damaged in auto accidents and those of people who died of contagious diseases. If the body is accepted, it will be embalmed using a special process to preserve it without refrigeration. Medical or dental students will then use the body for anatomical study. After about a year, the medical school will have the body cremated and the remains returned to you.

HOW WILL ARRANGEMENTS BE MADE?

You have three choices. You can use a funeral home or a memorial society, or you can do it yourself. Here are the pros and cons of each method.

FUNERAL HOMES

Most people naturally turn to a funeral home for help. The process of disposing of a body may seem so strange, complicated, and difficult that they want the services of an expert. But remember that a funeral home is a contractor. It is a business that sells goods and services relating to the disposition of bodies, and it will also provide you with all sorts of ancillary services from filing obituary notices to printing thank-you cards. As with all contractors, these services come at a price. The goods are marked up, and the services are sold at a substantial hourly rate.

As a result of massive fraud, deception, and overcharging in the 1960s and 1970s, legislation was passed in the 1980s to govern funeral home activities. Funeral homes are, for example, no longer able to aver, as they once did, that embalming is required. Embalming, the process of replacing bodily fluids with a preservative, is necessary if the body is to be held for many days, for example for a viewing. But if burial or cremation is to be immediate, there is no need for this process. Funeral homes are also required to provide prices over the phone or a written price list if requested. The latter can be faxed to you.

Here is an example of the range of services provided by funeral homes, along with representative prices. We sampled funeral homes across the country and found that the prices for all goods and services were remarkably similar.

Dressing: Dressing the body in clothing you provide, and applying cosmetics for viewing; $335

Providing clothing: $110

Embalming: $225

Refrigeration for overnight storage: $50 per 72 hours

Use of facilities and staff for viewing: $285

Use of facilities and staff for funeral: $535

Use of facilities and staff for memorial service: $465

Use of hearse: $185 plus $1 per mile over 25 miles

Register books, acknowledgment cards, envelopes: $49 to $114

But that is not all. Funeral homes across the country also tack on a special surcharge for the use of their services, which can range from $480 at a funeral home in Colorado to $585 in Florida to $1,889 in Connecticut. This includes the fee for talking to you about what services you want, preparing the death certificate, assisting with Social Security forms, "coordinating" with the cemetery—and, of course, your share of the funeral home's overhead costs. This fee will be charged regardless of whatever other goods or services you choose. There is also a range of other charges for special circumstances, for example, charges for preparation for shipping if the body must be transported from one location to another.

You can, if you wish, circumvent all discussion by buying a package plan. One funeral home, for example, has a list of services it calls the

"Simplicity Plan." The three options range from $2,395 for a chapel or church funeral service to $2,185 for a graveside funeral service to $1,770 for a less elaborate graveside memorial service. The advantage of using a funeral home is convenience. The disadvantage is expense.

MEMORIAL SOCIETIES

Memorial societies are essentially buying cooperatives. They were first formed in the 1930s, during tough economic times, in response to high funeral prices. They don't provide any goods and services themselves. Rather, they negotiate with local funeral homes to provide a basic burial or cremation. Memorial societies use their buying power—some have thousands of members—to negotiate better deals.

Memorial societies also educate their members about what kinds of goods and services are truly needed. Most of the savings come from encouraging members to buy only the products and services they actually need. One memorial society in Georgia, for example, offers, through six local funeral homes, a burial for $1,115. It includes a simple plywood casket, removal of the body from the home or hospital to the funeral home, dressing the body and putting it into the casket, filing papers and arranging for a death certificate, and transportation of the body to the grave site. It does not include the cemetery plot, the cost of opening and closing the grave, embalming, or the use of the facilities for memorial or committal services, all of which cost extra.

Every state has a memorial society. Most memorial societies ask that people join ahead of time, though family members can join on behalf of their deceased loved ones and avail themselves of services immediately. The cost is about $15 to $30. Memorial societies are staffed by volunteers, who also assist with such things as living wills and predeath planning. A major focus of memorial societies is to encourage members to make arrangements before they actually need them.

DOING IT YOURSELF

Believe it or not, it is entirely possible to handle a funeral and burial yourself. What's more, in rural areas, it's also still possible to bury a body at home on property you own. But to carry out arrangements yourself, certain things are required: you must obtain a death certificate, you must obtain a permit to transport a body, and you must check zoning laws regarding burial. There are several organizations that will assist you in planning such tasks. The definitive book on this subject is *Caring for Your Own Dead* by Lisa Carlson, published by Upper Access Publishers in Hinesburg, Vermont, and widely available in libraries.

A CASKET OR A COFFIN?

A casket or coffin is a container that holds the body for viewing and transport and that encases it for burial or cremation. There are many choices available, from downright cheap to outrageously expensive. The least expensive option, perhaps, is to build a casket yourself. What is a casket, after all, but a simple box? Indeed, in early American history the term "pine box" was almost synonymous with "casket." The book *Dealing Creatively with Death* by Ernest Morgan contains detailed instructions on such construction. Funeral homes also offer the inexpensive option of a cloth-covered wooden container for as little as $300. Or, if you are choosing cremation, you can select an even simpler container—a stiff cardboard box that will be incinerated along with the body.

If you are holding a viewing and need a casket for the purpose, many funeral homes will rent one. It is less expensive than buying a casket, but this option can cost money, too. Perhaps because so many people would otherwise avail themselves of this service, funeral homes have made rentals pricey as well. One funeral home, for example, quotes a price of $600 for rental of a casket for a two-day viewing and funeral service.

The cost of buying a casket from a funeral home can range from about $500 to more than $15,000. The difference is in the quality of the materials and workmanship of both the exterior and interior. They may be wood or metal; they may have waterproof seals and lengthy guarantees. But the fact is that a coffin is a consumer item in which the person it is intended for—the deceased—will take no pleasure whatsoever. As for you, the purchaser, you will be seeing your purchase for at most about seventy-two hours. There may be many reasons to buy a casket, but you should be sure that they justify the expense.

WHERE WILL THE REMAINS RESIDE?

Whether you choose burial or cremation, you will need to select a final resting place for the body or ashes. Here are your choices.

CREMATION

With cremation, you have two choices that cost little or nothing. You can scatter the ashes, or you can keep them in a container wherever you wish. Containers are available from funeral homes and suppliers of grave items. They can be simple or elaborate, but just about any container will do. Some people seal the ashes of a loved one in a beautiful vase and keep them at home. Scattering can be done at just about any location you choose. There may be local ordinances prohibiting it. But whether there are or not, you should scatter ashes quickly and discreetly. You may also choose to bury ashes. Special containers for this purpose are available from funeral homes or suppliers of grave items. The details of site selection and maintaining the grave are similar to those discussed below for the burial of a body.

If you choose to store the ashes, you can purchase a niche in what is called a "columbarium." Columbariums are owned and operated by churches or for-profit organizations, and the cost of a niche varies widely. Niches in less crowded areas are, of course, less expensive than those in high-demand urban areas. So a niche can cost anywhere from $600 to $700 all the way up to $3,000 for a space in a columbarium in northern Manhattan. Another factor governing the cost of a niche is its placement within the columbarium. Eye-level space is at a premium, while spaces closer to the ceiling or the floor, which are harder to see, are less expensive.

BURIAL

For burial of a body, you must first purchase a plot in a cemetery. Such a purchase has many of the same characteristics as a real estate transaction. What you are buying, however, is not a piece of land but rather the right to inter a body on land owned by someone else. Cemeteries can be owned by churches or municipalities, or they can be private for-profit ventures. Veterans of the armed forces also have the option of burial in one of the nation's military cemeteries.

Aside from military cemeteries, which are available free to veterans, the price of a cemetery plot, like the price of a piece of real estate, depends largely on location. First, there is the location within the country; prices are, of course, higher in more densely populated areas. Second is the location within the cemetery itself: the more attractive the spot, the more costly the plot. The size of the plot and its proximity to other grave sites are also factors in the price.

In a rural area, an ordinary burial plot may cost as little as $100. In an urban area, it may cost $3,000, occasionally even more for a scenic site. In one midsized metropolitan area, the average price for burial plots runs about $1,350. In this cemetery, lakeview plots cost just about double the average, or about $2,500. If you are planning on visiting the site frequently, you may wish to purchase a plot in a location that is pleasant and evocative for you.

The cost of the plot, however, is only the beginning. Most cemeteries require the additional purchase of a burial vault. This is a concrete liner into which the casket is dropped. It prevents the soil from sinking in around the casket. A concrete liner can cost between $200 and $4,000, depending on the materials and the construction. In addition, a cemetery will charge anywhere between $200 and $1,000, depending on local labor costs, to open and close the grave. And there will also be an annual fee for upkeep of the plot, unless there is a provision for "perpetual maintenance" in the purchase contract.

When you are selecting a cemetery, keep these important factors in mind:

- If you intend to visit frequently or even occasionally, how easy is it for you to reach?
- What types of markers are allowed? Some cemeteries allow only markers that are flush with the ground.
- What are the visiting hours?
- How good is the upkeep at the cemetery? Does it look well tended?
- What is the annual fee for upkeep? Does it seem reasonable in light of your local labor costs?
- If you plan on interring other family members, will there be space available?

Above-ground interment in a vault in a mausoleum is also an option. As with niches for cremated remains, mausoleum space is priced according to its location within the building. Eye-level space is the most costly.

HOW WILL THE GRAVE BE MARKED?

Grave markers run the gamut from a simple, earth-level bronze plaque to a substantial marble edifice, and prices vary accordingly. A bronze plaque, flush with the ground, will cost just over $1,000, on average. It is about twenty inches by fourteen inches in size, is mounted on a granite or marble square, and has a granite or marble base.

A standard granite headstone costs about $3,000. It is a granite block two feet high and four feet wide with lettering on one side, mounted on a six-foot-wide base. Elaborate carving or a long inscription will add to the cost. Black and red marble headstones are more expensive. In addition, the monument company or cemetery will charge a fee for mounting the stone in place that will vary according to local labor costs.

CHECKLIST FOR PLANNING A FUNERAL

____ Will you chose cremation or burial?

____ Who will arrange the funeral?

- A funeral home?

- A memorial society?

- Yourself?

____ What services do you need?

- Embalming?

- Clothing and cosmetics for viewing?

- Overnight refrigeration?

- Transport for the body:
  - From location of death to funeral home?
  - From funeral home to church or chapel?
  - From church or chapel to gravesite?
  - From location of death to crematorium?

____ What legal help do you need?

- Filing Social Security forms?
- Obtaining death certificates?
- Getting a permit to transport the body?

____ What other services will you need, and who will provide them?

- Memorial books?
- Placement of obituary?

____ What will you do with the remains?

- Cremate them?
- Scatter the ashes?
- Keep the ashes at home?
- Keep the ashes in a columbarium?
- Bury the body?

____ What kind of container will you use?

- A wood or metal casket?
- A simple plywood box?
- A cardboard container for cremation?
- A container for ashes?

____ What kind of cemetery plot do you need?

—— What other purchases will you need to make?

- Charge to crematorium?

- Grave vault?

- Opening and closing of the grave?

—— What kind of marker will you choose?

ACKNOWLEDGMENTS

The authors would like to thank everyone who so generously shared their experiences in planning memorial services for their friends and relatives.

We would also like to thank the clergy who collectively spent hours explaining the traditions of their denominations. These include Robert Lee, First Congregational Church, Burlington, Vermont; Craig Bustrin, Saint Michael's Episcopal Church, New York; Vince Rossi; Dr. Joseph L. Roberts, Ebenezer Baptist Church, Atlanta; Ted Wardlaw, Central Presbyterian Church, Atlanta; and John Weston, All Souls Unitarian Universalist Church, Kansas City, Missouri.

In addition, we would like to thank our agent and friend Mike Cohn. We would also like to extend our thanks to our editor, Frederic Hills, for being, as usual, the most professional, exacting, and thoughtful of editors; to Burton Beals for his deft touch; and to Hilary Black for her patience and efficiency.